TRANSFORMING BANGLADESH'S PARTICIPATION IN TRADE AND GLOBAL VALUE CHAINS

MAY 2023

Co-publication of the Asian Development Bank and Islamic Development Bank Institute.

ISDBI
معهد البنك الإسلامي للتنمية
Islamic Development Bank Institute

ADB

Notes:
1. In this publication, "$" refers to United States dollars.
2. ADB recognizes "Vietnam" as Viet Nam.

Cover design by Joe Mark Ganaban.

On the cover: (*Left*) Trainee learns knitting at a training center, run by Bangladesh Garment Manufacturers and Exporters Association, in Tongi near Dhaka. (*Middle*) Female workers in Wool Tex Sweaters Limited in Shewrapara in Dhaka. (*Bottom middle*) Trucks carry goods unloaded from ships in the Chittagong Port. (*Top right*) Singaporean ship in Chittagong Port. (*Bottom right*) Workers monitor the production process at the Programme for Rural Advancement Nationally (PRAN) factory. PRAN is Bangladesh's largest food and nutrition company was founded in 1980 (photos by Abir Abdullah).

CONTENTS

TABLES, FIGURES, AND BOXES

Boxes

FOREWORD

Bangladesh has made considerable progress during the 5 decades since its independence in 1971. From being one of the poorest countries in the world, it has shown steady improvements in poverty reduction, job creation, and the living conditions of its people. Today, Bangladesh's gross domestic product is larger than Denmark's and Singapore's and is already higher than that of neighboring India and Pakistan on a per capita basis. This remarkable transformation was partly fueled by Bangladesh's successful entry into global value chains (GVCs), with the country eventually becoming the world's second largest supplier of clothing.

Bangladesh prides itself on making and exporting ready-made garments. After all, the industry supports millions of livelihoods and brings substantial income and investments to the economy, which consequently has pulled many out of poverty. But the economy's dependence on this sector has started to show signs of vulnerability. Deep specialization in garments means that sources of future growth could be limited. Export competitiveness could erode as the economy matures and reaches the limits of its trade privileges. Reliance on exports also does not bode well in a world economy where shocks are becoming more frequent and severe. For example, when the coronavirus disease (COVID-19) pandemic struck, Bangladesh's garment sector suffered tremendously. A large portion of the workforce, mostly women, lost their jobs as factories closed. Looking ahead, addressing these vulnerabilities and other structural issues will be necessary for achieving Bangladesh's aspiration to become an upper-middle income country by 2031.

The Asian Development Bank (ADB) and the Islamic Development Bank Institute (IsDBI) have embarked on a knowledge collaboration to understand how GVCs can be effectively leveraged as a tool for development. With the broad aim of closing the data and knowledge gaps on the impact of GVCs on developing economies, the collaboration has already produced two reports: *The Evolution of Indonesia's Participation in Global Value Chains,* published in October 2019; and *Pakistan's Economy and Trade in the Age of Global Value Chains*, published in January 2022.

The same objectives motivated the writing of this report, which focuses on Bangladesh's expanding role in the global economy. Titled *Transforming Bangladesh's Participation in Trade and Global Value Chains,* this report assembles and analyzes data on the structure of Bangladesh's economy and its links with the rest of the world. Unique in this report for Bangladesh are chapters that assess trade agreements and the economy's potential for diversification and transformation, which are in line with the country's development strategies. What emerges from the study is an evolving picture of Bangladesh's trade patterns arising from its long-held comparative advantage in a few industries. The report finds that the economy can build on its recent success by unlocking productivity gains from technology adoption, narrowing the digital divide, and broadening participation in GVCs. This report also identifies high-potential industries with deeper domestic linkages that offer opportunities for broadening the base of economic growth. It concludes by emphasizing the need to strengthen human capital, attract productive investments, address infrastructure gaps, and modernize trade policy structures to encourage economic diversification.

We hope that the wealth of data and insights collected in this report can serve as a valuable reference for policymakers and analysts seeking to understand various facets of Bangladesh's economy. We would like to congratulate the ADB and IsDBI officials and consultants involved in producing this key analytical product and affirm our continued support for this knowledge collaboration.

Albert Park
Chief Economist and Director General,
Economic Research and Regional Cooperation Department,
Asian Development Bank

Sami Al-Suwailem
Acting Director General,
Islamic Development Bank Institute and
Chief Economist,
Islamic Development Bank Group

ACKNOWLEDGMENTS

This report makes extensive use of the Asian Development Bank's (ADB) flagship statistical product—the multiregional input–output tables (MRIOTs)—to study the state and evolution of Bangladesh's participation in globalized production processes. It is an output of the collaborative knowledge initiative between ADB and the Islamic Development Bank Institute (IsDBI) on global value chains and is designed to serve as a technical reference for analysts and policymakers at a time when economic globalization is facing headwinds.

We gratefully acknowledge the leadership provided by ADB's chief economist and director general Albert Park and acting director general of IsDB Institute and chief economist of IsDB Group Sami Al-Suwailem in this knowledge collaboration. We also thank Edimon Ginting and Joseph Ernest Zveglich, Jr. of ADB for guiding the work; and Muhammad Sulaiman (IsDB Regional Hub Dhaka), Bukhari Sillah, Muhamed Zulkhibri, Abu Camara, Mohamed Elgoussi, Novia Budi Parwanto, Ali Rashed, Abdul Rashid, Jahm Mae E. Guinto (consultant) of IsDBI for reviewing the study. Valuable insights and feedback from Zaidi Sattar, Rana Hasan, Pramila Crivelli, and Soon Chan Hong enhanced the quality of the analysis, as did comments from participants of the Asian Impact Webinar on Transforming Bangladesh's Participation in Trade and Global Value Chains. We also acknowledge the support of our data partners, official statistics agencies, and ADB-IsDBI common members participating in our joint statistical and analytical capacity-building initiatives.

This report was written by Janine Elora Lazatin and Karishma Banga under the direct supervision of Mahinthan Joseph Mariasingham, with inputs from Julian Thomas Alvarez, Cherryl Chico, Ma. Charmaine Crisostomo, Christian Regie Jabagat, Angelo Jose Lumba, Leila Rahnema, and Eric Suan. Many of the indicators featured in this report were computed using the ADB MRIOTs which are compiled and maintained by Michael John Barsabal, John Arvin Bernabe, Julieta Magallanes, Sarah Mae Manuel, and Ana Francesca Rosales. We also acknowledge the consortium of research institutes headed by the University of Groningen for permitting the use of the data from the World Input–Output Database (WIOD).

Joy Quitazol-Gonzalez edited the publication. The cover was designed by Joe Mark Ganaban who also led the typesetting process. Eric Suan organized and coordinated the preparation of this report. The publishing team in ADB's Department of Communications and Office of Administrative Services Logistics Management Unit (Printing) provided general guidance on production issues.

Elaine S. Tan
Advisor, Office of the Chief Economist and Director General,
and Head, Statistics and Data Innovation Unit,
Economic Research and Regional Cooperation Department
Asian Development Bank

Areef Suleman
Director
Economic Research and Statistics
Islamic Development Bank Institute

ABBREVIATIONS

ADB	–	Asian Development Bank
ADB-MRIOT	–	ADB Multiregional Input–Output Table
B2C	–	business-to-consumer
CEPII	–	Centre d'Etudes Prospectives d'Informations Internationales (the main French institute for research into international economics)
COVID-19	–	coronavirus disease
CPTPP	–	Comprehensive and Progressive Agreement for Trans-Pacific Partnership
DAVAX	–	directly absorbed value-added exports
DAVAX1	–	DAVAX by importers through final goods
DAVAX2	–	DAVAX by importers through intermediate goods
DDS	–	digitally deliverable services
DVA	–	domestic value-added
EBA	–	Everything but Arms (European Union)
EU	–	European Union
FDI	–	foreign direct investment
FVA	–	foreign value-added
GDP	–	gross domestic product
GSP	–	Generalized System of Trade Preferences
GVA	–	gross value-added
GVC	–	global value chain
HHI	–	Herfindahl–Hirschman Index
HS	–	Harmonized System
ICT	–	information and communication technology
LDC	–	least developed country
NEC	–	not elsewhere classified
NRCA	–	normalized revealed comparative advantage
PDC	–	pure double counting
PRC	–	People's Republic of China
RCA	–	revealed comparative advantage
RCEP	–	Regional Comprehensive Economic Partnership
REF	–	reflection; value-added exports that are reexported by the direct importer and eventually absorbed by the origin economy
REX	–	value-added exports that are reexported by the direct importer and finally absorbed abroad
RMG	–	ready-made garments
TFP	–	total factor productivity
UK	–	United Kingdom
UN	–	United Nations
US	–	United States
WBES	–	World Bank Enterprise Survey

HIGHLIGHTS

This statistical analysis report provides a comprehensive review of Bangladesh's economy from the perspective of the country's participation in global value chains (GVCs) as it transitions into a developing country. It uses the most recent information alongside cutting-edge methods in data analysis. The report uncovers patterns and trends in GVC participation; unpacks the pursuit of diversification, agglomeration, and digitalization; and provides an evidence-based narrative to support economic analysis and policymaking.

Macroeconomy and Exports

- Bangladesh's remarkable accomplishments in economic growth and poverty reduction were driven in large part by the ready-made garments (RMG) sector. The contribution to gross domestic product (GDP) of the agriculture sector, which was once the economy's major source of income, has declined by almost 50 percentage points since the early 1970s because of the rising share of industry, which reached 33% in 2021.

- Although Bangladesh's role in international merchandise trade has been quite limited, a closer look into its textiles sector reveals that it played a significant role in global trade, even becoming the second largest exporter next to the People's Republic of China. Bangladesh's exports are also dominated by textile products, but the gradual rise in contributions of other sectors such as post and telecommunications has resulted in a declining share of textiles in exports.

- Compared to its competitors, Bangladesh emerged as the most concentrated in terms of exports, indicating a relatively high specialization toward specific products in the textiles sector. Although there has been a tendency toward diversification in recent years, concentration was still higher in 2020 than in the early 2000s.

- Bangladesh fell below the world average in terms of trade openness despite the significance of its RMG sector in global exports. The economy also lagged its competitors such as Cambodia, India, Pakistan, and the People's Republic of China. Thus, increasing the international trading activities of its other sectors presents as a viable option for attaining further growth.

Participation in Global Value Chains

- Decomposing gross exports into value-added terms shows a clear orientation toward direct trading. RMG exports of Bangladesh are mostly ready for final consumption, thereby not requiring further processing except for distribution to stores. On the other hand, the foreign value-added content of gross exports has been increasing, indicating more backward integration—that is, Bangladesh's industries are becoming more reliant on imports.

- The United States, Germany, and the United Kingdom were the top destinations for Bangladesh's exports, with textile products dominating the trade. The list of top recipient economies was still the same regardless of whether the content of Bangladesh's exports was dominated by domestic or foreign value-added.

- The report uses two metrics to gauge GVC participation. The first is a trade-based approach that takes the share of indirect trade in gross exports, while the second is a production-based approach that uses the share of domestic value-added in intermediate exports to the total domestic value-added created by an economy. Bangladesh's GVC participation rates were relatively low, falling below the world average by around 20 percentage points. Further, backward participation has also outweighed forward participation throughout the years, implying that Bangladesh was located at more downstream stages of the GVCs it participates in.

- Average production lengths also offer valuable insights into the role of economies in GVCs. Forward average production lengths pertain to the average number of steps separating domestic value-added creation in intermediates to its final consumption. Backward average production lengths refer to the average number of steps between the first use of foreign value-added in intermediates as primary inputs until its final consumption. The forward to backward ratio gives the GVC position of an economy or economy-sector, with values above (below) 1 indicating relative upstreamness (downstreamness).

- For Bangladesh, a gradual increase in the aggregate average forward and backward GVC lengths was seen over 2000–2021. From a sector point of view, there was variability in trends. Many manufacturing sectors saw declining forward GVC lengths while all but two sectors (renting of machinery and equipment, and other business services) exhibited increasing backward GVC lengths.

- Bangladesh's GVC position was relatively downstream compared to the world average throughout the 2000–2021 period. Against its competitors, however, the economy was relatively upstream up until 2013, before moving the other direction in subsequent years. Although the relative position of Bangladesh's textiles sector was generally more downstream, a convergence toward the world average has been observed since 2019. During the same period, however, its counterparts in competitor economies moved further upstream.

Diversification, Specialization, and Agglomeration

- Although not direct exporters, certain domestic sectors make value-added contributions to the production of export-oriented output. However, standard gross trade-based approaches are inadequate to discern such indirect yet crucial intersector dependencies. This report, employing advanced statistical frameworks and cutting-edge methods, bridges such analytical gaps, thereby facilitating more complete economic and policy analyses.

- Export diversification is a key policy priority for Bangladesh. One metric used to operationalize this concept is the Herfindahl-Hirschman Index (HHI) which measures the degree of concentration. Bangladesh's HHI using gross exports was significantly higher than the HHI using value-added exports, suggesting that the economy is more diverse than shown by traditional analysis.

- From the value-added-based analysis, it is also seen that Bangladesh was more on par with its competitors like Cambodia and Pakistan in terms of export concentration. Even though the textiles sector still comprised a major share of value-added exports, a more balanced distribution was observed with sectors such as agriculture, wholesale, post and telecommunications, finance, and other business services making larger contributions to export production.

- The revealed comparative advantage (RCA) indices based on gross and value-added exports were used to assess the specialization or competitiveness of Bangladesh's sectors. Regardless of which measure is used, the economy exhibited comparative advantage in six sectors: (i) textiles and textile products; (ii) post and telecommunications; (iii) leather, leather products, and footwear; (iv) public administration and defense; compulsory social work; (v) construction; and (vi) manufacturing, not elsewhere classified. Five more sectors showed comparative advantage when considering only value-added exports, underlining the importance, for economic and policy analyses, of discerning the extent of domestic sector linkages of export-oriented industries. The five sectors are (i) agriculture, hunting, forestry and fishing; (ii) other community, social, and personal services sector; (iii) finance; (iv) other nonmetallic minerals; and (v) inland transport.

- In 2021, for Bangladesh, the textiles sector showed the highest RCA, followed by the post and telecommunications sector. However, the advantage dampened when the more preferred value-added exports were considered instead of gross exports. There were considerable variations in RCA trends across many sectors when gross export-based estimates were compared with valued-added-based ones. Some sector measures differed in terms of the pace of change, while others showed trend reversals.

- Agglomeration captures how much value added is sourced from and/or absorbed by domestic sectors relative to the rest of the world. Bangladesh was a high agglomeration economy over the 2000–2021 period, with the value-added contribution of domestic sectors to its final products consistently higher than the world average and the value-added generated from within primarily consumed locally. Although the economy's overall level of agglomeration did decline between 2007 and 2014, it increased thereafter indicating decreasing GVC participation.

- Bangladesh's textiles sector exhibited low levels of agglomeration between 2000 and 2021, because of its relatively low reliance on domestic sources of intermediates and the country's limited intermediate or final consumption of the value-added generated by it. It is noteworthy that the textiles sector in Viet Nam and Cambodia also showed low agglomeration. Interestingly, while sector backward and forward agglomeration for the two economies declined over time, Bangladesh's generally exhibited a positive trend—indicating the domestic economy's increasing contribution to the production and consumption of outputs of the textiles sector.

Least Developed Country Graduation, Preference Erosion, and Geographical Diversification

- For Bangladesh, along with its impending graduation in November 2026 from a status of least developed country comes the challenge of discontinuation of benefits granted by preferential trading schemes. With more favorable rules of origin being established in 2011 as part of the Everything but Arms agreement, substantial increases in the European Union (EU)-based preference utilization immediately followed, and, for example, textile products exported to the EU amounted to $17.3 billion by 2021. Thus, considerable amount of export-driven income is being threatened by the imminent erosion of preferences.

- The geographical breakdown of Bangladesh's exports reveals apparent concentration toward the EU economies. This can be sustained beyond its graduation by applying for other preferences under the union such as the Special Incentive Arrangement for Sustainable Development and Good Governance. As an alternative, Bangladesh can diversify its export destinations and expand market access by entering into new treaties such as regional trade agreements. Recently enforced regional trade agreements include the Regional Comprehensive Economic Partnership (RCEP) and the Comprehensive and Progressive Agreement for Trans-Pacific Partnership (CPTPP).

- Alternative destinations of the heavily concentrated exports of Harmonized System (HS) 61 (apparel and clothing accessories; knitted or crocheted) and HS 62 (apparel and clothing accessories; not knitted or crocheted) can be determined by identifying top destinations and alternative markets for each. Unsurprisingly, top destinations of Bangladesh's HS 61 and HS 62 exports were mostly from the EU. The US remained as the first export market destination for HS 62 products despite the absence of trade preferences. Japan—a member of both the RCEP and CPTPP—was also one of the main recipients.

- The leading importers of Bangladesh's HS 61 and HS 62 products also happened to be the top export destinations among economies that are dependent on imports for these products. Alternative markets for HS 61 include Japan, Poland, Russian Federation, Switzerland, and Austria. A similar set of economies are possible alternative destinations for HS 62 exports with the inclusion of members of the RCEP and CPTPP, namely the Republic of Korea and Australia, respectively. Existing realities and legislation, which include possible losses in trade preferences from these alternative markets, are important to factor in when assessing the viability of trade redirection.

Digitalization and Economic Transformation

- Analysis of firm survey data finds that digitalized (i.e., those using emails and/or have a web presence) manufacturing firms had higher total factor productivity and export intensity compared with their nondigitalized counterparts. Thus, a positive relationship between digitalization and structural transformation is observed in the firm-level survey data.

- Digitalization rates, which measure the adoption of digital technologies and automation, varied significantly across Bangladesh's sectors. These were highest for "digital industries" such as information services; telecommunications; and computer, electronic, and optical equipment. The air transport, coke and refined petroleum, electrical machinery and apparatus, pulp and paper products, and rubber and plastic products sectors also registered relatively better rates. The digitalization rate of Bangladesh's textiles sector at 0.95% was higher than the rates of its competitors, Maldives, Pakistan, and Sri Lanka; although, it was significantly lower than India's (3.28%).

- RMG manufacturing-led economic growth could potentially face further challenges in the future with the expected rise in wages, continued suspension of export orders for public health and safety concerns, and the accelerating digital development. Such pressures call for modifications to the current pattern of economic transformation in Bangladesh, which include export diversification, targeting foreign direct investment inflows, and furthering digitalization of firms.

- While noticeable increases in industrial labor productivity in Bangladesh were observed in recent times, significant variation exists across sectors. Industrial labor productivity was higher than services and agricultural productivity in 2019. Decomposing labor productivity growth into structural change and a "within-sector" component reveals that the within-sector component drives the positive changes observed in Bangladesh. However, the contribution of structural change to economic growth has been increasing noticeably over time.

- Despite the relatively high share of Bangladesh's manufacturing products in its total merchandise exports, the country's export basket consisted mostly of low complexity goods, reflecting the current low value-adding, downstream role of the textiles sector in GVCs. In terms of economic complexity, Viet Nam's transformation provides important lessons for Bangladesh—a transformation that was driven by targeting foreign direct investments and regional production networks in sectors and products that offer high potential.

- Increasing the export contribution of the leather and leather footwear sector presents as a viable and promising step for diversification, given its growth, investment, and employment-creating potential. Manufacturing economies specializing in RMG have been shown to specialize more easily in footwear because of the close link between the textiles sector and the leather and leather footwear sector.

- Bangladesh continued to have lower total Internet penetration, fixed broadband access, and Internet bandwidth compared with its competitors. In addition, e-commerce only accounted for 0.2% of its gross domestic product due in large part to the high cost of data and poor postal reliability in the economy.

- The textile and wearing apparel sector accounted for roughly 25.2% of Bangladesh's inbound FDI in 2022. On the other hand, the leather and leather products, telecommunications, as well as computer software and IT services sectors, which could facilitate diversification towards higher complexity exports, only accounted for 3.0%, 5.2%, and 1.0% of FDI inflows, respectively, in the same year.

- It is noteworthy that, as per the survey, Bangladesh was quite advanced in the use of more sophisticated sewing machines compared to Viet Nam. Furthering the scope of digitalization to include other functions such as payments and sales, as well as arrangements for shipping and distribution, can potentially bring Bangladesh up to par with its competitors in the global RMG market.

Chapter 1
INTRODUCTION

Bangladesh prides itself on its ready-made garments (RMG) sector. This sector has helped the economy achieve fast growth, reduce poverty, achieve economic and social development, and provide the population with jobs while also engendering women empowerment through employment opportunities. Its success in the RMG sector is an inspiring story of an economy that took steps to harness its comparative advantage, develop the capacities needed, and innovate policies to successfully embed itself in world trade when the opportunity presented itself (Sattar 2022).

While Bangladesh benefited much from its participation in the RMG trade, it can be argued that it may be time for further economic transformation and diversification. The economy still benefits from having a large working-age population that can be tapped for labor supply. This is the same advantage it had in the 1980s when Bangladesh's RMG industry was at its nascent stages. Additionally, Bangladesh benefits from having the experience in reforming policy to help open the economy to trade. This has happened for the RMG sector and can also happen for the other sectors. Although conditions have changed and are expected to change further with the economy's graduation from least developed country (LDC) status, there is still considerable potential for Bangladesh to expand its role in trade and global value chains (GVCs), as this report will show.

This publication combines data from various sources to weave a story of Bangladesh's macroeconomy and gross exports, participation in GVCs, competitiveness, and potential for diversification and transformation. Chapter 2 uses data from the Asian Development Bank (ADB), Centre d'Etudes Prospectives d'Informations Internationales (CEPII), the International Monetary Fund, and the World Bank to describe Bangladesh's macroeconomy and role in exports.

In Chapter 3, GVC indicators published by ADB are used to analyze Bangladesh's participation in global value chains. GVC indicators are derived by applying decomposition techniques on the ADB Multiregional Input–Output Tables (ADB-MRIOTs) for 2000 and 2007–2021. A schematic of the ADB-MRIOTs is drawn in Figure 1.1.

The ADB-MRIOTs contain input–output information for 35 sectors in 62 economies and a residual "rest of the world." Intermediates use and exports matrices, along with vectors for value-added, final demand, and total output, from the ADB-MRIOTs can be used to derive value-added export components that are better able to account for and describe today's nature of trade, where production is fragmented across several borders and value-added crosses borders multiple times. This chapter uses the techniques proposed by Borin and Mancini (2019) and Wang et al. (2017a and 2017b), among others, to decompose gross exports into value-added terms and determine GVC participation, lengths, and positions.

Figure 1.1: A Schematic Representation of the ADB Multiregional Input-Output Table

		Economy A	...	Rest of the World	Economy A	...	Rest of the World	Total Output
		c1 ... c35	...	c1 ... c35	c1 ... c35	...	c1 ... c35	
Economy A	c1 ⋮ c35							
⋮	⋮			Z			Y	x
Rest of the World	c1 ⋮ c35							
Value-added		va						
Total Output		x						

Source: Asian Development Bank. Multiregional Input–Output Database (accessed 21 July 2022).

There are several statistics and indicators that can be used to analyze the role of domestic sectors in a GVC setting and the role that GVCs play in enhancing domestic sector linkages. These statistics will be discussed in Chapter 4, which focuses on an economy's diversification, specialization and competitiveness, and agglomeration while taking into account local production activities. This chapter will make use of value-added exports to assess diversification, following Bajaj et al. (2022), revealed comparative advantage, and agglomeration following Mercer-Blackman, Foronda, and Mariasingham (2017) and Baris et al. (2022).

The importance of trade agreements and preferential treatments comes into play for Bangladesh as it nears its graduation from LDC status. Existing trade agreements are explored in Chapter 5 using data from the United Nations Conference on Trade and Development (UNCTAD) Database on Generalized System of Trade Preferences (GSP) Utilization. The loss of preferential treatment as Bangladesh transitions to middle-income country status also highlights the importance of exports diversification both from a product perspective and a geographical perspective. Chapter 5 explores both these dimensions using data from the United Nations (UN) Comtrade Database by employing the methodology proposed by Crivelli (2022). It suggests alternative economies with whom Bangladesh can strengthen trade through negotiations of new trade agreements.

Chapter 6 deep dives into several aspects of transformation and diversification in Bangladesh. It presents new analysis on economic transformation and digitalization in Bangladesh using data from the economic transformation database of the United Nations University World Institute for Development Economics Research, the International Telecommunication Union dashboard, and the World Bank Enterprise Surveys (WBES). Following McMillan, Rodrik, and Verduzco-Gallo (2014), economic transformation is defined as the process of (i) moving toward higher productivity sectors ("between-sector" growth or structural change) and (ii) improving productivity within a sector ("within-sector" growth). The decomposition of labor productivity growth for Bangladesh shows that the within-sector component of labor productivity growth is driving economic transformation in the country, but the structural change component has been increasing and growth-enhancing. There is much potential for a digital-led economic transformation through enhanced productivity and export intensity. Bangladesh needs to leverage digital technologies to enable export diversification in targeted manufacturing sectors, such as the leather, leather products, and footwear sector, where it enjoys a strong competitive advantage but lags on digitalization.

Finally, Chapter 7 concludes the report by laying out recommendations based on the analyses presented in previous chapters. Policies that helped Bangladesh succeed in RMG can be models for further policy reforms to promote transformation and diversification.

Chapter 2
MACROECONOMY AND EXPORTS

Bangladesh is a well-known economy for its exemplary macroeconomic growth and poverty reduction performance. From being among the poorest nations at its independence in 1971, Bangladesh graduated to lower-middle-income status in 2016. Throughout the decades, Bangladesh saw positive and increasing economic growth, with the momentum only slowing after the coronavirus disease (COVID-19) pandemic in 2020 (Figure 2.1).

Figure 2.1: Bangladesh Real Gross Domestic Product Growth Rate, 1980–2027 (%)

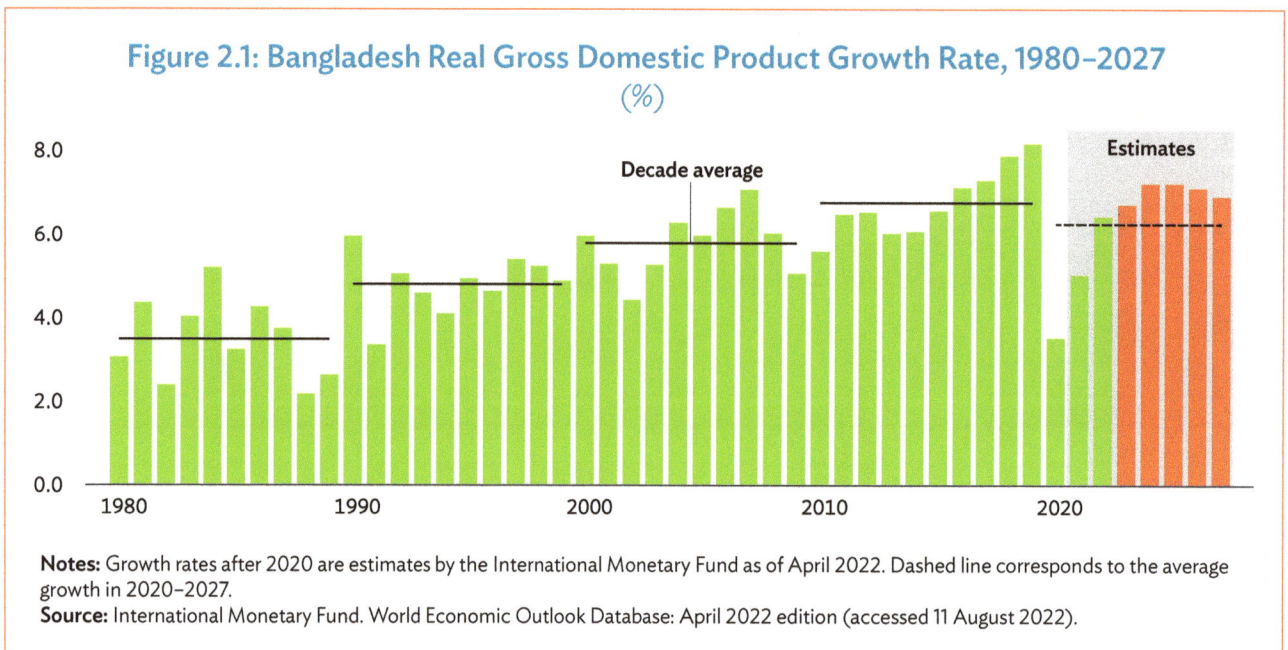

Notes: Growth rates after 2020 are estimates by the International Monetary Fund as of April 2022. Dashed line corresponds to the average growth in 2020–2027.
Source: International Monetary Fund. World Economic Outlook Database: April 2022 edition (accessed 11 August 2022).

In the 1980s, growth was volatile due in part to political instability. Nevertheless, data from the International Monetary Fund (2022) shows that Bangladesh managed to grow at an average of 3.5% per year during the 1980s. The economic reforms and the boom in industry in the 1990s allowed the economy to increase growth by 1.3 percentage points to 4.8% per annum on average. Political uncertainties in the 2000s posed challenges to growth, yet the booming industrial sector allowed the economy to grow by an average of 5.8% per year in the 2000s and 6.8% per year in the 2010s. Growth in 2020 was affected by the COVID-19 pandemic, but Bangladesh managed to pose positive growth for the year, in contrast to many other economies that experienced economic contractions. While recovery is expected in the aftermath of the pandemic, international geopolitical instability and macroeconomic conditions are expected to hamper growth, resulting in slower forecasted growth in Bangladesh for 2020–2027.

Among Bangladesh's growth drivers is its highly successful integration into the ready-made garments (RMG) sector. The RMG sector in Bangladesh paved the way for the transformation of the economy from an agricultural economy to one with a significant share of industry. Data from the World Bank (2022) shows that, in 1972, agriculture accounted for 59.6% of gross domestic product (GDP), while industry accounted for less than 6.1% of GDP. By 2021, the share of agriculture in GDP went down to 11.6%, while the share of industry has grown to 33.3%. Moreover, the development of the RMG sector allowed Bangladesh to participate actively in world trade and global value chains (GVCs).

The Centre d'Etudes Prospectives d'Informations Internationales-Basis for International Trade Analysis (CEPII-BACI) International Trade Database merchandise exports trade values and quantities data shows that Bangladesh plays a small role in total international merchandise trade, accounting for only 0.2%–0.3% of total merchandise exports for 2016–2020. However, the economy accounts for 5.2% of textiles and textile products sector merchandise exports and competes with Viet Nam as the second largest exporter of total products within that sector, next to the People's Republic of China (PRC) (Figure 2.2.b). Bangladesh's most prominent trade links are with European economies and the United States (US), as shown by the black lines highlighted in Figures 2.2.a and 2.2.b. These relatively larger exports to Germany, the US, and the United Kingdom (UK) are driven by Bangladesh's apparel exports to these economies.

The importance of the RMG sector for the Bangladesh economy can likewise be seen in its trade data. Figure 2.3.a shows a breakdown of the economy's total exports using the Asian Development Bank Multiregional Input–Output Tables (ADB-MRIOTs); whereas, Figure 2.3.b presents Bangladesh's merchandise exports data by broad product groupings from the CEPII-BACI. The ADB-MRIOTs consider total exports, including services exports, while the CEPII-BACI trade data focuses on merchandise exports. In both instances, there is a clear dominance of the textile and textile products sector and in Bangladesh's exports. Figure 2.3.a shows that, since 2000, the textiles and textile products sector has been the largest single contributor to exports. However, its share has since decreased in favor of the other sectors, such as post and telecommunications. The textiles and textile products sector's share amounted to 84.8% of total gross exports in 2000, 80.1% in 2010, 77.6% in 2019, and 74.8% in 2021.

In contrast, the CEPII-BACI dataset in Figure 2.3.b shows that a large and growing portion of Bangladesh's merchandise exports is in textile products and footwear. In 2002, textile products and footwear accounted for 88.3% of the economy's total merchandise exports, with apparel and clothing accessories accounting for 78.5% of total merchandise exports. By 2020, textile products and footwear accounted for 94.0% of total merchandise exports, with apparel and clothing accessories accounting for 85.5% of total merchandise exports.

Figure 2.2: Global Merchandise Exports Network, 2016–2020

a. Total Merchandise Exports

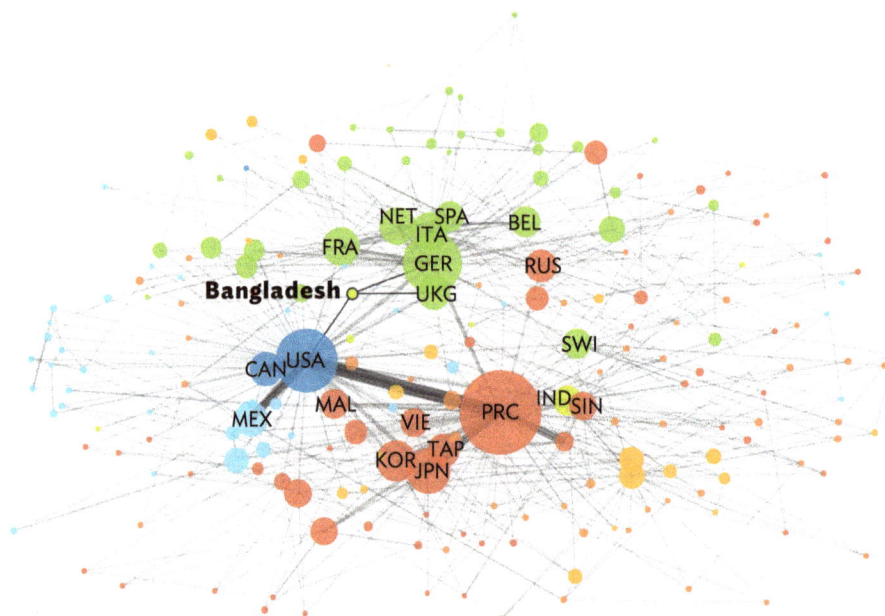

b. Textiles and Textile Products Sector Merchandise Exports

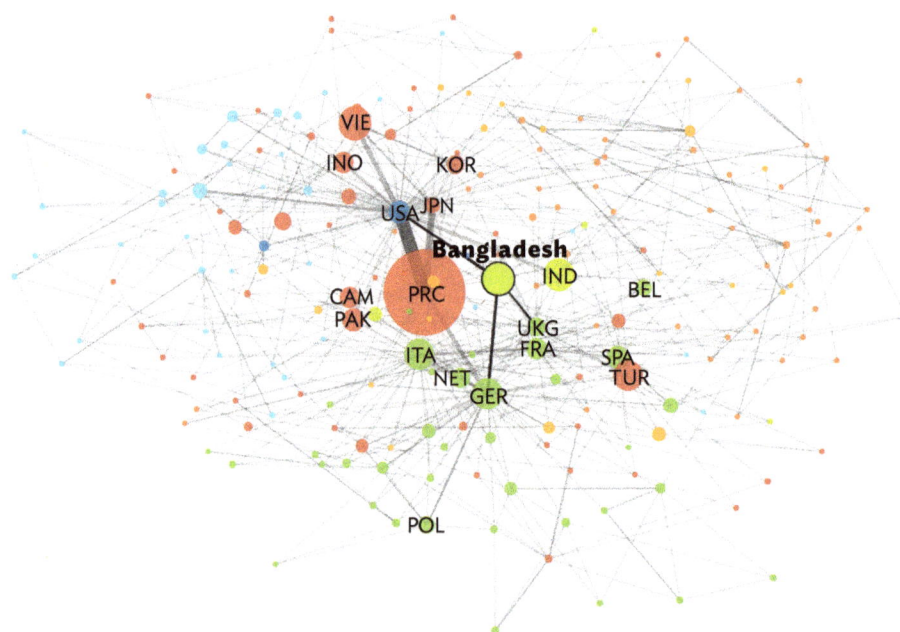

BEL = Belgium; CAN = Canada; FRA = France; GER = Germany; IND = India; ITA = Italy; JPN = Japan; KOR = Republic of Korea; MAL = Malaysia; MEX = Mexico; NET = Netherlands; PRC = People's Republic of China; RUS = Russian Federation; SPA = Spain; SIN = Singapore; SWI = Switzerland, Liechtenstein; TAP = Taipei,China; UKG = United Kingdom; USA = United States of America; and VIE = Viet Nam.

Notes: Each node represents an economy, while node size indicates the relative size of exports. Node colors are used to represent the regions to which economies belong. Edges include only the top three links of each economy, and their size represents the size of exports. Edges for Bangladesh are colored black for emphasis. Textiles and textile products sector merchandise exports are computed by mapping merchandise exports from the Centre d'Etudes Prospectives d'Informations Internationales (CEPII)-BACI database into the appropriate Asian Development Bank Multiregional Input–Output Table (ADB-MRIOT) sectors.

Source: CEPII. BACI International Trade Database (accessed 21 July 2022).

Figure 2.3: Breakdown of Gross Exports, Bangladesh, Various Years
(%)

a. Exports by Sector, 2000, 2007–2020

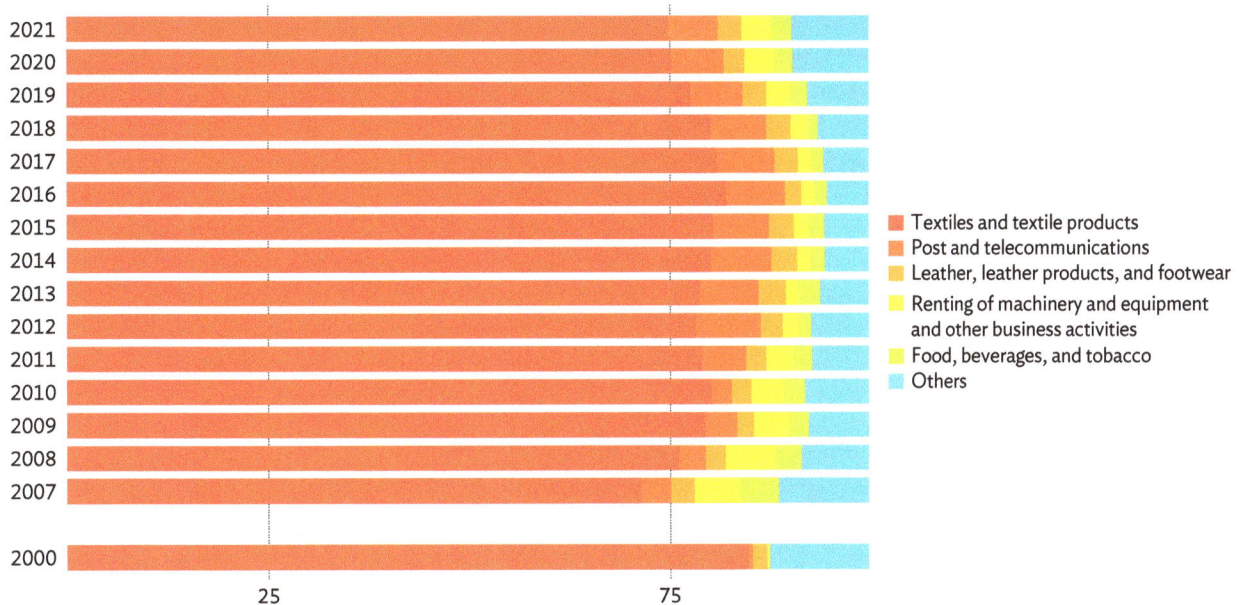

Legend:
- Textiles and textile products
- Post and telecommunications
- Leather, leather products, and footwear
- Renting of machinery and equipment and other business activities
- Food, beverages, and tobacco
- Others

Source: Asian Development Bank (ADB). 2021. *Key Indicators for Asia and the Pacific 2021*. Manila; ADB. Multiregional Input–Output Database (accessed 14 July 2022); and ADB estimates.

b. Merchandise Exports by Broad Product Groupings, 2002–2020

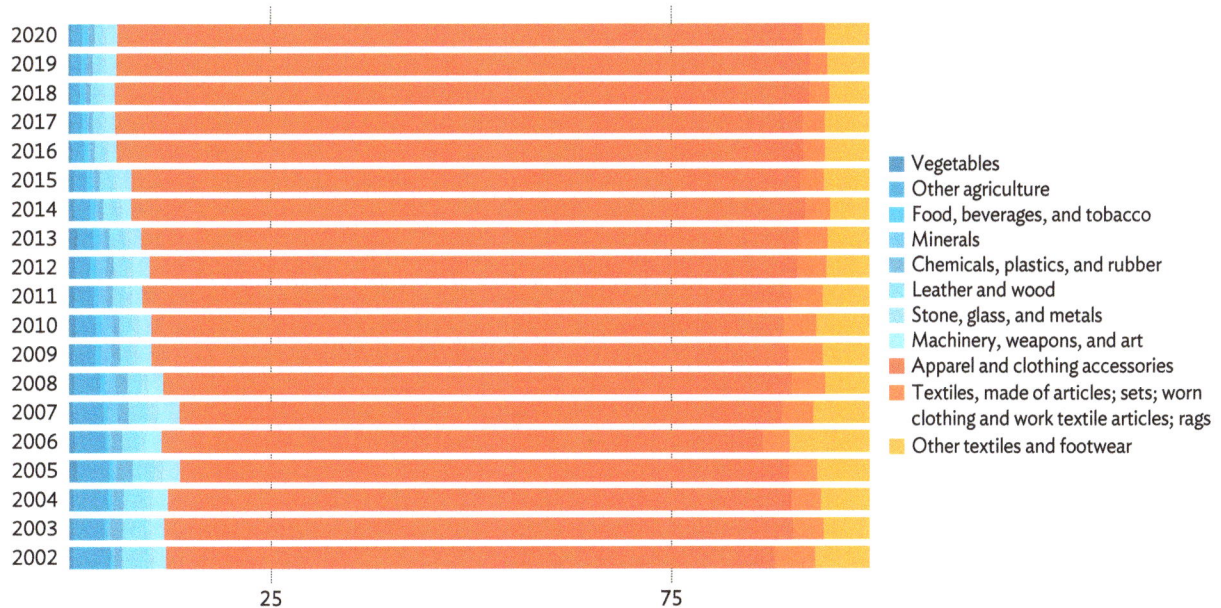

Legend:
- Vegetables
- Other agriculture
- Food, beverages, and tobacco
- Minerals
- Chemicals, plastics, and rubber
- Leather and wood
- Stone, glass, and metals
- Machinery, weapons, and art
- Apparel and clothing accessories
- Textiles, made of articles; sets; worn clothing and work textile articles; rags
- Other textiles and footwear

Notes: Broad product groupings are based on the chapters of the Harmonized System, 2002 edition. "Vegetables" covers 06–14. "Other agriculture" covers 01–05 and 15. "Food, beverages, and tobacco" covers 16–24. "Minerals" covers 25–27. "Chemicals, plastics, and rubber" covers 28–40. "Leather and wood" covers 41–49. "Textiles and footwear" covers 50–67. "Stone, glass, and metals" covers 68–83. "Machinery, weapons, and art" covers 84–97. Within "Textiles and footwear," "Apparel and clothing accessories" covers 61 and 62; "Textiles, made of articles; sets; worn clothing and work textile articles; rag" covers 63; and "Other textiles and footwear" covers 50–60 and 64–67.
Source: Centre d'Etudes Prospectives d'Informations Internationales (CEPII). BACI International Trade Database (accessed 21 July 2022).

This concentration of Bangladesh's exports is reflected in diversification indexes, such as the Herfindahl–Hirschman Index (HHI).[1] Figure 2.4 uses the CEPII-BACI dataset at the two-digit level of the 2002 revision of the Harmonized System (HS) of commodity classification to show how Bangladesh fares in diversification compared with its competitors in textile product exports. Note that the higher the HHI, the more concentrated an economy is. Bangladesh emerged as the most specialized economy among its competitors, and increasing concentration has been seen throughout the years. Meanwhile, economies like Cambodia and India have diversified. Other economies that saw increasing concentration are the PRC and Viet Nam, although their main exports have shifted to electronics. Pakistan, whose exports also rely largely on textile products, is more diverse than neighboring Bangladesh.

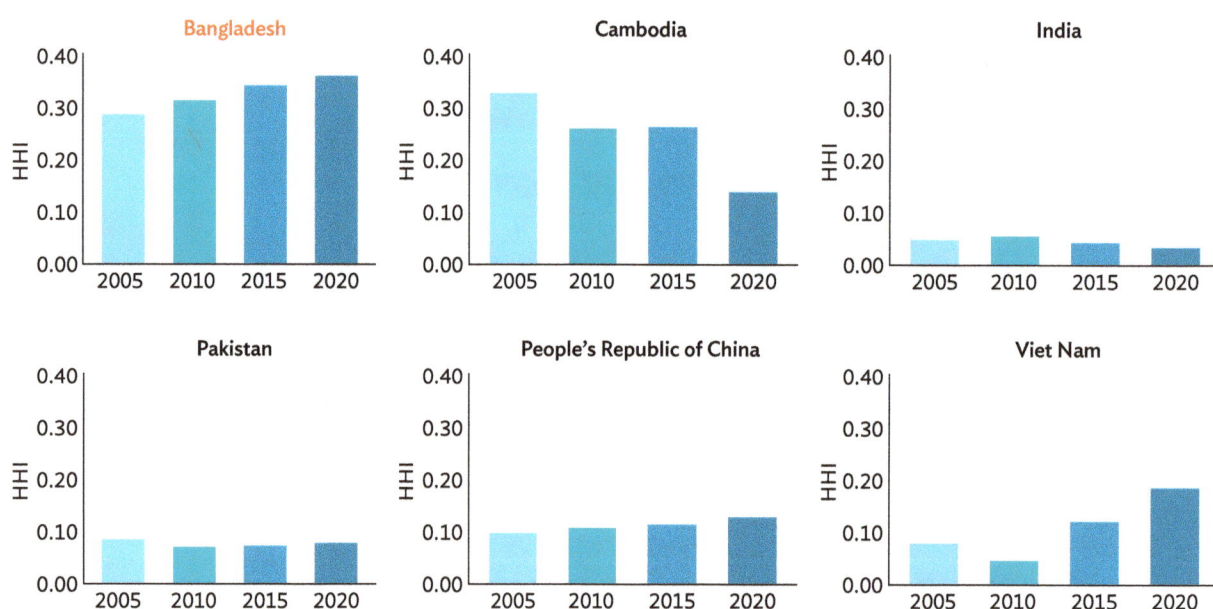

Figure 2.4: Merchandise Export Diversification, Selected Economies, 2005, 2010, 2015, 2020

HHI = Herfindahl-Hirschman Index.
Notes: Diversification is measured by the normalized HHI. A higher index indicates a lower level of diversification. Products are disaggregated at the two-digit level of the Harmonized System, 2002 edition.
Sources: Centre d'Etudes Prospectives d'Informations Internationales (CEPII). BACI International Trade Database (accessed 21 July 2022); and Asian Development Bank estimates.

Figure 2.5 uses the formula for HHI (footnote 1) to compute for diversification within the textiles and textile products sector.[2] It first maps merchandise exports data from the CEPII-BACI into corresponding ADB-MRIOT sectors, and then calculates a diversification index for each sector. There are two things to note from Figure 2.5. First, it shows that concentration on specific products within the textiles and textile products sector in Bangladesh increased from 2002 to 2008 and followed a trend of growing diversification

---

[1]   The HHI is computed by taking the square of each product's share in an economy's merchandise exports and then summing these squares up. It is normalized by subtracting one over the number of active product lines in the economy from the sum of squared shares, and then dividing this by one minus one over the number of active product lines in the economy.

[2]   Product lines at the six-digit level were mapped to the ADB-MRIOT sectors to understand diversification within a sector.

since 2009. However, exports within the textiles and textile products sector in Bangladesh is still more concentrated in 2020 than in 2002. Although the number of six-digit HS 2002 revision product lines mapped into the textiles and textile products sector has increased from 2002 to 2020 in Bangladesh, fewer product lines take up larger shares of exports, resulting in a higher HHI index. Second, Bangladesh shows the highest concentration in the sector among competitors, indicating a relatively increased specialization within certain product lines of the textiles and textile products sectors—particularly RMG—compared with other big exporters in the sector.

Figure 2.5: Herfindahl–Hirschman Index of the Textiles and Textile Products Sector Using Merchandise Exports, Selected Economies, 2002–2020

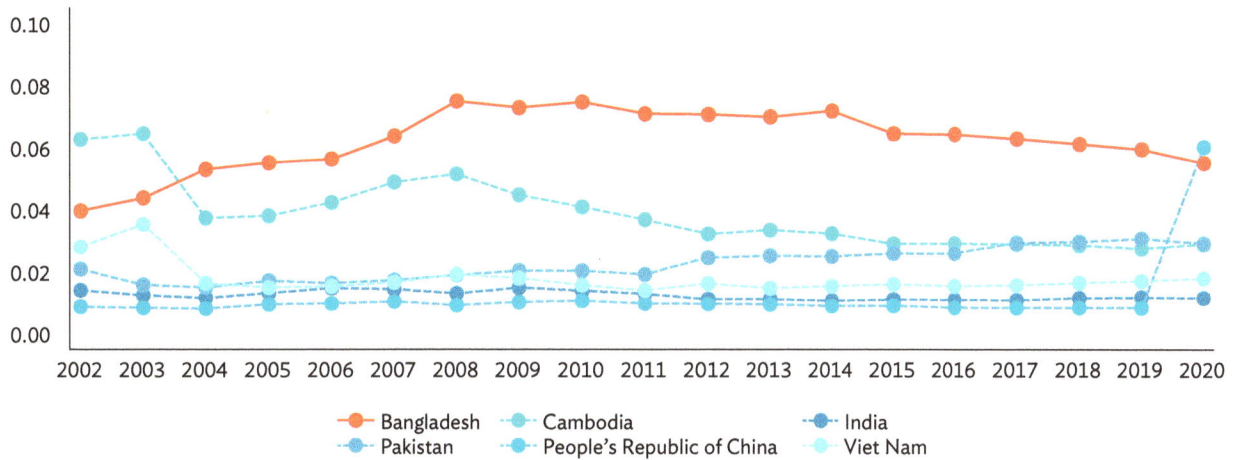

Notes: The formula for the Herfindahl–Hirschman Index (HHI) is used to compute for a sector's export diversification. A higher HHI indicates a lower level of diversification.
Sources: Centre d'Etudes Prospectives d'Informations Internationales (CEPII). BACI International Trade Database (accessed 21 July 2022); and Asian Development Bank estimates.

Despite the significance of the RMG sector in Bangladesh's trade and economy, a comparison with other economies suggests that Bangladesh can further expand its trade openness to achieve growth. Figure 2.6 uses data from the World Bank World Development Indicators database to map trade openness (imports and exports as a percentage of GDP) against economy size or GDP. Blue markers indicate economies of about the same size as Bangladesh, green markers indicate other significant apparel exporters, and the orange marker is used to highlight Bangladesh. The negatively sloping black line in the plot draws a linear regression fitted line. Figure 2.6 shows that, given Bangladesh's size, the economy falls below the average in terms of trade openness. The economy's trade openness also falls below competing economies like Cambodia, India, Pakistan, and the PRC. Indeed, 2021 data from the World Bank World Development Indicators shows that Bangladesh has the third lowest share of imports and exports to GDP at only 27.7%, higher than only Ethiopia (24.3%) and Sudan (4.1%). Thus, there is space to increase the economy's trade openness.

Figure 2.6: Trade Openness at Various Levels of Economic Development, 2021

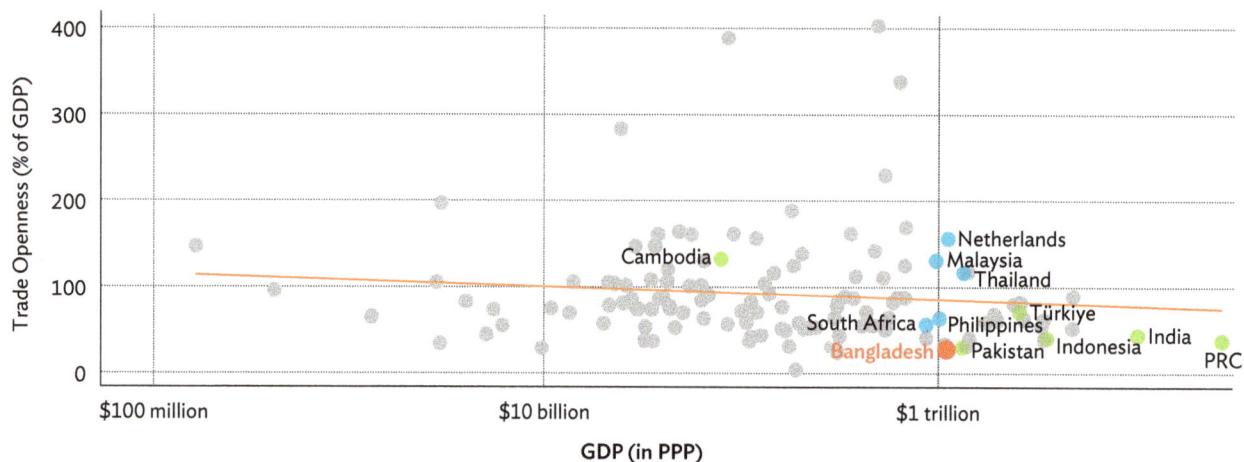

GDP = gross domestic product, PPP = purchasing power parity, PRC = People's Republic of China.
Notes: The horizontal axis is GDP in current international dollars at PPP, transformed using a base 10 log scale. The vertical axis is the sum of exports and imports of goods and services as a share of GDP. Blue nodes refer to economies of similar economic size to Bangladesh, while green nodes refer to economies competing with Bangladesh in the exports of apparel. The black negatively sloping line in the plot is a linear regression fitted line.
Source: World Bank. World Development Indicators (accessed 21 November 2022).

The macroeconomic data presented in this chapter show the high concentration of Bangladesh in the textiles and textile products sector, specifically in the RMG sector. While exports from this sector can be partially credited to Bangladesh's stellar economic growth performance, its eventual graduation from the UN's least developed countries (LDCs) list in 2026 poses future challenges to the sector. Graduation from LDC status would mean the loss of certain privileges and support measures designed for LDCs. Thus, countermeasures are needed to mitigate the possible impacts of graduation and for Bangladesh to meet its vision of becoming an upper-middle-income economy by 2031.

One strategy Bangladesh can pursue to fuel future growth is increasing its exports. This can be done by developing other export sectors, as it had successfully done for the RMG sector in the 1980s. One way to expand its exports is for Bangladesh to increase its participation in GVCs. The fragmented production structure associated with GVCs allows economies to participate in only specific production segments of different sectors without needing to build entire chains locally. With the right policies, economies participating in GVCs can take advantage of technology transfers embedded in foreign value-added while also learning to increase their efficiency and competitiveness in selected sectors. Moreover, participation in GVCs can create jobs and increase employment, helping to improve the earnings and living standards of populations.

Chapter 3

PARTICIPATION IN GLOBAL VALUE CHAINS

Advancements in logistics and information and communication technology (ICT), coupled with more liberalized trade, have given rise to the fragmentation of production across several borders. Such an arrangement allows firms to relocate parts of production in economies with comparative advantage in these tasks or specific endowments that enable them to produce more efficiently at lower prices.

From statistical and policy perspectives, however, the fragmentation of production in global value chains (GVCs) poses several challenges. Existing accounting frameworks record gross exports, resulting in double counting of trade, as GVCs usually entail multiple back-and-forth trades to create a single product (Ahmad 2019). Export decomposition frameworks applied to input–output tables have been developed to help policymakers paint a better picture of the nature of trade within the context of GVCs.

This chapter will use the frameworks developed by Borin and Mancini (2019) and Wang et al. (2017a and 2017b) to draw a picture of Bangladesh's GVC participation, length, and position. The primary data source for these computations is the Asian Development Bank Multiregional Input–Output Tables (ADB-MRIOTs) for 2000 and 2007–2021, which feature input–output data for 62 economies and 35 sectors. A residual economy is also included as "rest of the world." This chapter will also use ADB's published GVC indicators uploaded to the ADB Multiregional Input–Output Database to analyze trends and patterns of GVCs in Bangladesh and comparator economies.

A.   Exports Decomposition

A good starting point for analyzing GVCs in Bangladesh is to use the Borin and Mancini (2019) export decomposition technique as simplified in ADB (2021b) (Figure 3.1). This framework decomposes gross exports into several value-added terms, beginning with directly absorbed value-added exports (DAVAX). DAVAX comprises the value-added exports that are directly absorbed by importers through final goods (DAVAX1) or intermediate goods (DAVAX2). In this case, the value-added only goes through one border, crossing from the origin economy. The second term is domestic value-added exports that are reexported by the direct importer and finally absorbed abroad (REX). The third term is reflection, composed of value-added exports that are reexported by the direct importer and eventually absorbed by the origin economy (REF). Note that REX and REF cross borders more than once. DAVAX, REX, and REF make up total domestic value-added, or value-added that originated domestically from the exporting economy. Foreign value-added (FVA), makes up the fourth term of the decomposition. It is the total of all value-added originating from foreign sources that are embedded in an economy's gross exports. The fifth and final term is pure double counting (PDC). It refers to the value-added that is counted multiple times and crosses the same border more than once.

Figure 3.1: Decomposing Exports into Value-Added Categories

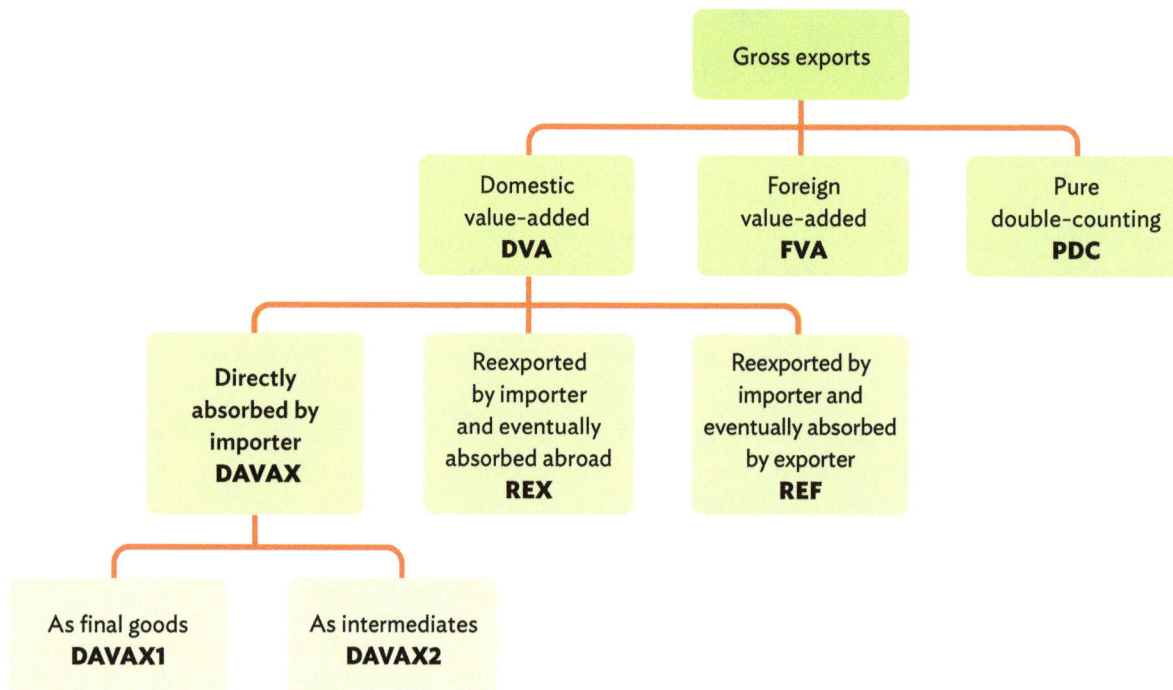

Source: Asian Development Bank. 2021. *Key Indicators for Asia and the Pacific 2021*. Manila.

Figure 3.2 decomposes Bangladesh's gross exports into the five value-added categories, as in Borin and Mancini (2019). Data shows that from 2000 to 2021, about 69.8%–77.4% of Bangladesh's gross exports comprise DAVAX. While this share has slowly declined from 77.4% in 2000 to 74.5% in 2021, it still makes up a large portion of gross exports excluded from GVCs under a trade-based approach, as in Hummels, Ishii, and Yi (2001) and Borin and Mancini (2019). DAVAX, or direct trading, is significant in Bangladesh because of the products driving its exports. Ready-made garments (RMG) are generally final goods usually needing no further processing except to distribute them to stores, hence the high DAVAX component in exports.

The remaining terms in the decomposition make up indirect trade or GVC under a trade-based approach. The REF and PDC terms in Bangladesh have insignificant contributions to gross export. Meanwhile, the share of REX in gross exports has experienced peaks and troughs throughout the periods considered. In 2000, REX was recorded at 9.2% of gross exports. It peaked at 12.3% during the height of the global financial crisis in 2008, dropped to 9.2% the following year, and climbed back up to 12.2% in 2013. The share of REX declined again the next year before reaching 12.1% in 2016. Subsequently, the share of REX declined, ending at 4.3% of gross exports by 2021, less than half of its share in 2000.

FVA, on the other hand, followed a generally increasing trend, indicating that Bangladesh is steadily becoming more backward integrated. The share of FVA in gross exports was only at 13.4% in 2000 but climbed to a peak of 24.8% in 2018 before settling at 21.2% in 2021. In total, indirect trading, as measured by the sum of REX, REF, FVA, and PDC, ranged from a low of 22.6% in 2000 to a peak of 30.1% in 2018. Data for 2021 shows that this share was at 25.5%.

Figure 3.2: Decomposition of Bangladesh Exports into Value-Added Categories, 2000, 2007–2021
($ billion)

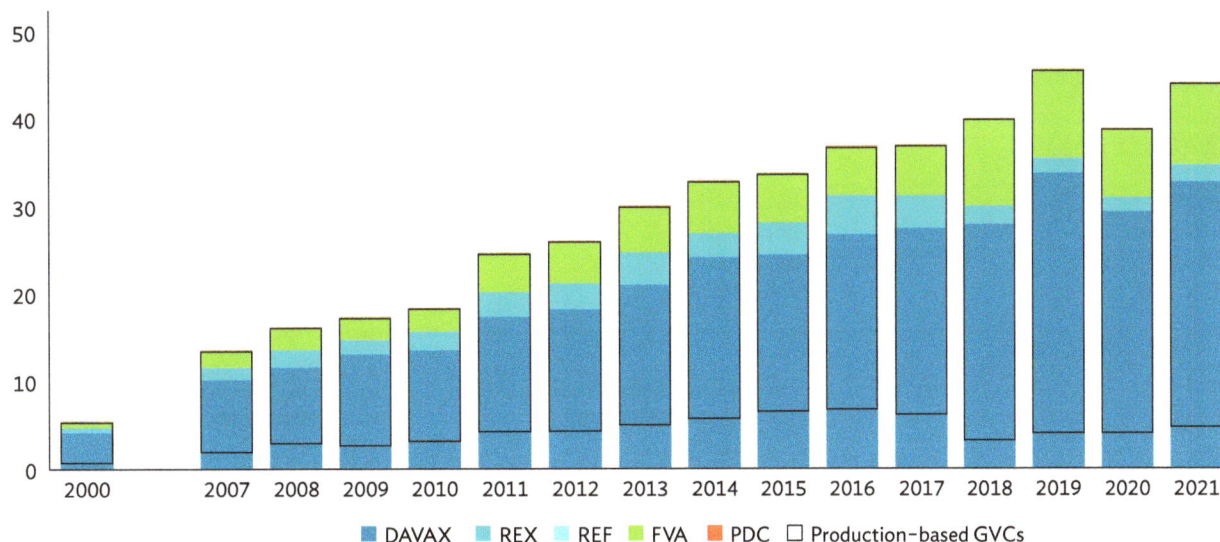

GVC = global value chain.
Notes: Gross exports are decomposed using the methodology in Asian Development Bank (2021), following Borin and Mancini (2019). DAVAX are directly absorbed domestic value-added exports. REX are domestic value-added exports reexported by direct importer and eventually absorbed abroad. REF are domestic value-added exports reexported by direct importer and eventually returned to and absorbed at home. FVA are foreign value-added embedded in gross exports. PDC are pure double counting, a result of value-added crossing the same border more than once. The boxed portions measure GVC production according to Wang et al. (2017).
Sources: Asian Development Bank (ADB). 2021. *Key Indicators for Asia and the Pacific 2021.* Manila; ADB. Multiregional Input–Output Database (accessed 14 July 2022); A. Borin and M. Mancini. 2019. Measuring What Matters in Global Value Chains and Value-Added Trade. *Policy Research Working Paper.* No. 8804. Washington, DC: World Bank; Z. Wang, S. Wei, X. Yu, and K. Zhu. 2017. Characterizing Global Value Chains: Production Length and Upstreamness. *NBER Working Paper.* No. 23261. Cambridge, MA: National Bureau of Economic Research; and ADB estimates.

GVC-related exports slightly improve when considering a production-based approach, as in Wang et al. (2017b). In this approach, DAVAX2, REX, REF, and FVA are considered part of GVC-related production, as represented by the boxed portion of the bars in Figure 3.2. This production-based GVC portion accounted for 32.3%–46.5% of gross exports and was higher during the global financial crisis in 2008 and in 2010–2017. Shares have since declined to levels seen in the 2000s.

Figure 3.3 shows the top 10 destinations of each value-added category for 2017–2021. The largest destination of Bangladesh's exports was the United States (US), accounting for 21.7% of total exports, followed by Germany (13.3%) and the United Kingdom (UK) (5.9%). The textiles and textile products sector made up 85.8% of exports to the US, 92.3% of exports to Germany, and 85.6% of exports to the UK. The top seven destinations for DAVAX were the same as in exports, but Japan ranked ahead of India in DAVAX, and Canada replaced Italy as the 10th largest destination of DAVAX. As with exports, the top export sector in the top three destinations is the textiles and textile products sector, which accounted for 84.2% of total DAVAX to the US, 92.5% of total DAVAX to Germany, and 85.7% of total DAVAX to the UK.

Figure 3.3: Top 10 Trading Partners of Bangladesh by Value-Added Category, 2017–2021
(%)

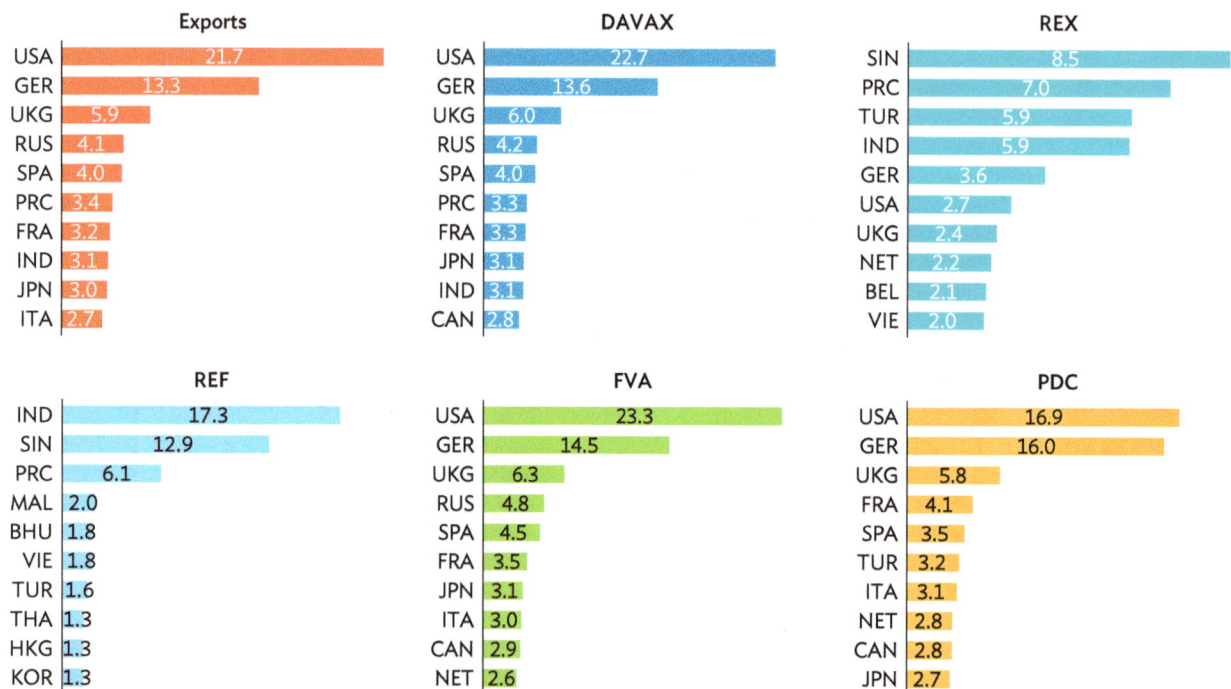

Exports

USA	21.7
GER	13.3
UKG	5.9
RUS	4.1
SPA	4.0
PRC	3.4
FRA	3.2
IND	3.1
JPN	3.0
ITA	2.7

DAVAX

USA	22.7
GER	13.6
UKG	6.0
RUS	4.2
SPA	4.0
PRC	3.3
FRA	3.3
JPN	3.1
IND	3.1
CAN	2.8

REX

SIN	8.5
PRC	7.0
TUR	5.9
IND	5.9
GER	3.6
USA	2.7
UKG	2.4
NET	2.2
BEL	2.1
VIE	2.0

REF

IND	17.3
SIN	12.9
PRC	6.1
MAL	2.0
BHU	1.8
VIE	1.8
TUR	1.6
THA	1.3
HKG	1.3
KOR	1.3

FVA

USA	23.3
GER	14.5
UKG	6.3
RUS	4.8
SPA	4.5
FRA	3.5
JPN	3.1
ITA	3.0
CAN	2.9
NET	2.6

PDC

USA	16.9
GER	16.0
UKG	5.8
FRA	4.1
SPA	3.5
TUR	3.2
ITA	3.1
NET	2.8
CAN	2.8
JPN	2.7

BEL = Belgium; BHU = Bhutan; CAN = Canada; FRA = France; GER = Germany; HKG = Hong Kong, China; IND = India; ITA = Italy; JPN = Japan; KOR = Republic of Korea; MAL = Malaysia; NET = Netherlands; PRC = People's Republic of China; RUS = Russian Federation; SPA = Spain; SIN = Singapore; THA = Thailand; TUR = Türkiye; UKG = United Kingdom; USA = United States; VIE = Viet Nam.
Notes: Gross exports are decomposed using the methodology in Asian Development Bank (2021), following Borin and Mancini (2019). DAVAX are directly absorbed domestic value-added exports. REX are domestic value-added exports reexported by direct importer and eventually absorbed abroad. REF are domestic value-added exports reexported by direct importer and eventually returned to and absorbed at home. FVA are foreign value-added embedded in gross exports. PDC are pure double counting, a result of value-added crossing the same border more than once.
Sources: Asian Development Bank (ADB). 2021. *Key Indicators for Asia and the Pacific 2021*. Manila; ADB. Multiregional Input–Output Database (accessed 14 July 2022); A. Borin and M. Mancini. 2019. *Measuring What Matters in Global Value Chains and Value-Added Trade. Policy Research Working Paper*. No. 8804. Washington, DC: World Bank; and ADB estimates.

REX shows a different set of top destinations, with Singapore, the People's Republic of China (PRC), and Türkiye being the top three destinations. Bangladesh's biggest exporting sectors of REX to Singapore were renting of machinery and equipment and other business services (44.8%) and post and telecommunications (26.5%). For the PRC, Bangladesh's biggest exporting sectors of REX were textiles and textile products (33.6%) and leather, leather products, and footwear (17.7%). Meanwhile, the textiles and textile products sector made up 95.1% of Bangladesh's REX to Türkiye.

Top FVA destinations for Bangladesh follow the same top five destinations of exports, but the succeeding five are different. For the top three destinations, the textiles and textile products sector made up 92.8% of total FVA from Bangladesh to the US, 95.9% of total FVA from Bangladesh to Germany, and 92.9% of total FVA from Bangladesh to the UK.

By sector, the textiles and textile products sector dominated exports and all value-added categories by a large margin for 2017–2021 (Figure 3.4). Except in PDC, it was followed by the post and telecommunications sector. Renting of machinery and equipment and other business services also appeared among the top five sectors for exports, DAVAX, REX, and REF; whereas, leather, leather products, and footwear appeared among the top exporting sector in exports, DAVAX, REX, FVA, and PDC. Food, beverages, and tobacco is a top exporting sector for exports, DAVAX, REF, FVA, and PDC. Public administration and defense was a top exporting sector for REX and REF, while manufacturing, not elsewhere classified (NEC) was a top exporting sector for FVA and PDC. Another thing to note is that REX and REF have less disproportionately distributed sector contributions than exports, DAVAX, FVA, and PDC.

Figure 3.4: Top Five Sectors in Bangladesh by Value-Added Category, 2017–2021 (%)

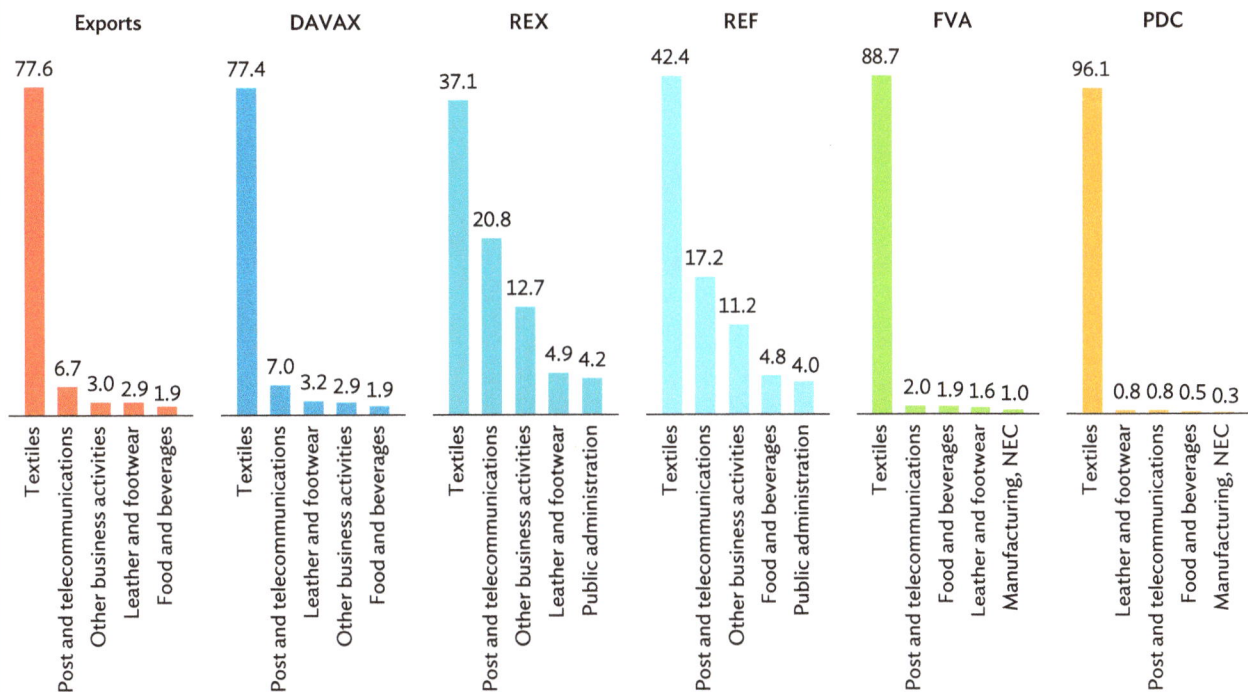

NEC = not elsewhere classified.

Notes: Gross exports are decomposed using the methodology in Asian Development Bank (2021), based on Borin and Mancini (2019). DAVAX are directly absorbed domestic value-added exports. REX are domestic value-added exports reexported by direct importer and eventually absorbed abroad. REF are domestic value-added exports reexported by direct importer and eventually returned to and absorbed at home. FVA are foreign value-added embedded in gross exports. PDC are pure double counting, a result of value-added crossing the same border more than once. Sector names are shortened according to Appendix 2.

Sources: Asian Development Bank (ADB). 2021. *Key Indicators for Asia and the Pacific 2021*. Manila; ADB. Multiregional Input–Output Database (accessed 14 July 2022); A. Borin and M. Mancini. 2019. Measuring What Matters in Global Value Chains and Value-Added Trade. *Policy Research Working Paper*. No. 8804. Washington, DC: World Bank; and ADB estimates.

B.   Global Value Chain Participation

GVC participation indexes can be calculated from exports decomposition. Under a trade-based approach, forward participation is the share of REX and REF to total exports, while backward participation is the share of FVA and PDC to total exports. Total GVC participation is then derived by adding forward participation and backward participation. The production-based forward participation rate, following Wang et al. (2017b), can be computed by getting the share of DAVAX2, REX, and REF to GDP (or sector gross value-added [GVA]) using a decomposition of exports by origin sector. Figure 3.5 presents the historical trends of these three GVC participation rates for Bangladesh.

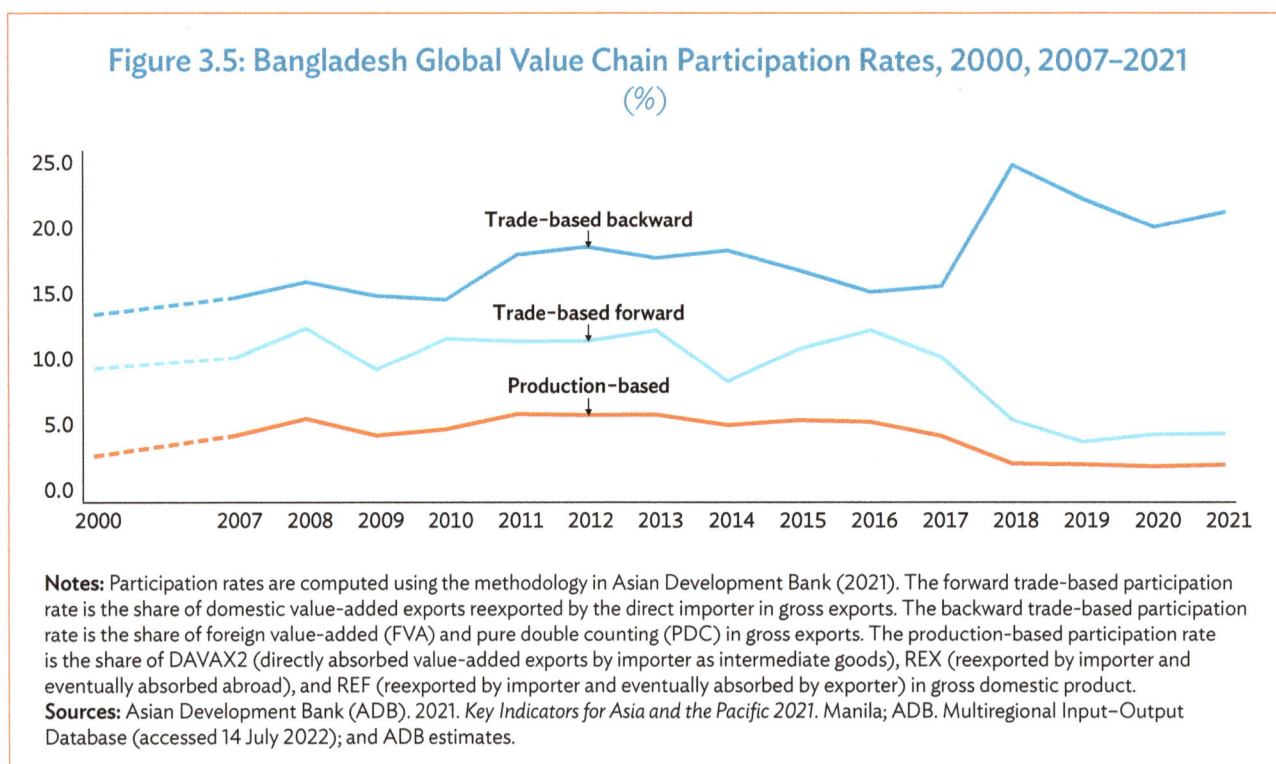

Figure 3.5: Bangladesh Global Value Chain Participation Rates, 2000, 2007–2021
(%)

Notes: Participation rates are computed using the methodology in Asian Development Bank (2021). The forward trade-based participation rate is the share of domestic value-added exports reexported by the direct importer in gross exports. The backward trade-based participation rate is the share of foreign value-added (FVA) and pure double counting (PDC) in gross exports. The production-based participation rate is the share of DAVAX2 (directly absorbed value-added exports by importer as intermediate goods), REX (reexported by importer and eventually absorbed abroad), and REF (reexported by importer and eventually absorbed by exporter) in gross domestic product.
Sources: Asian Development Bank (ADB). 2021. *Key Indicators for Asia and the Pacific 2021*. Manila; ADB. Multiregional Input–Output Database (accessed 14 July 2022); and ADB estimates.

Historical trends show that forward participation, whether measured through a trade-based or production-based approach, is lower than backward participation in Bangladesh. This would imply that Bangladesh is situated more downstream in the GVC chains. Higher FVA shares compared with REX, as shown in Figure 3.2, are driving this wedge between forward and backward participation. It must also be noted that the difference in backward and forward participation has widened since 2017, driven by the increasing FVA shares and declining REX shares in later years.

Figure 3.6 compares Bangladesh's GVC participation rates against other economies for 2000, 2010, and 2021. Compared with other economies, Bangladesh's participation rates are at the lower end. It recorded trade-based total GVC participation rates between 22.6% and 26.01%, far below the world average of between 40.6% and 46.0%. Bangladesh only fared better than Pakistan in trade-based total GVC participation rate and ranked last based on production-based GVC forward participation rate.

Figure 3.6: Global Value Chain Participation Rates of Selected Economies, 2000, 2010, and 2021
(%)

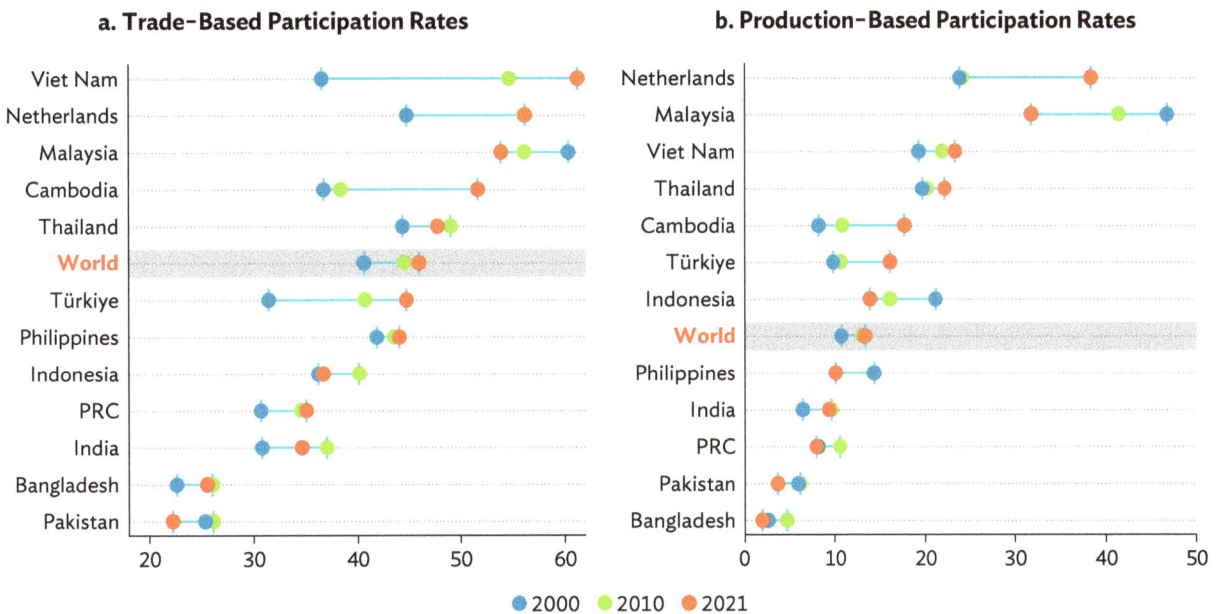

a. Trade–Based Participation Rates

b. Production–Based Participation Rates

● 2000 ● 2010 ● 2021

PRC = People's Republic of China.
Notes: Trade-based participation rates are computed using the methodology in Asian Development Bank (2021). The backward participation rate is the share of foreign value-added (FVA) and pure double counting (PDC) in gross exports, while the forward participation rate is the share of domestic value-added exports reexported by the direct importer in gross exports. The production-based participation rate is the share of DAVAX2 (directly absorbed value-added exports by importer as intermediates), REX (reexported by importer and eventually absorbed abroad), and REF (reexported by importer and eventually absorbed by exporter) in gross domestic product.
Sources: Asian Development Bank (ADB). 2021. *Key Indicators for Asia and the Pacific 2021*. Manila; ADB. Multiregional Input–Output Database (accessed 14 July 2022); Z. Wang, S. Wei, X. Yu, and K. Zhu. 2017. Measures of Participation in Global Value Chains and Global Business Cycles. *NBER Working Paper*. No. 23222. Cambridge, MA: National Bureau of Economic Research; and ADB estimates.

Compared with Viet Nam, which competes with Bangladesh as the second largest exporter of textiles and textile products, Bangladesh's GVC participation rates fell far behind. Viet Nam has vastly improved its trade-based participation rate by strengthening its GVC linkages in the other sectors, while Bangladesh's participation rate has stayed between 20% and 30%. Even in production-based participation rates, Viet Nam recorded rates between 19.3% and 23.4% in the periods considered, while Bangladesh's participation rate only ranged between 1.8% and 4.7%. Moreover, production-based participation also declined in 2021 compared to 2000 and 2010. These comparatively low participation rates imply that Bangladesh can still increase GVC participation as a strategy to increase exports.

Figure 3.7 decomposes Bangladesh's aggregate participation rates into 35 sectors for 2000, 2010, and 2021. First, it is easy to see that the aggregate participation rate hides variations in participation across sectors. The economy-wide participation rates in Bangladesh are heavily influenced by the textiles and textile products sector because of the magnitude of its exports as compared with the other sectors. Second, forward participation in the aggregate falls below backward participation, but this differs by sector. Thus, it pays to analyze sector-level participation rates to assess what sectors can do to increase participation in GVCs.

Figure 3.7: Bangladesh Global Value Chain Participation Rates by Sector, 2000, 2010, and 2021
(%)

a. Trade-Based Total Participation Rates

b. Production-Based Participation Rates

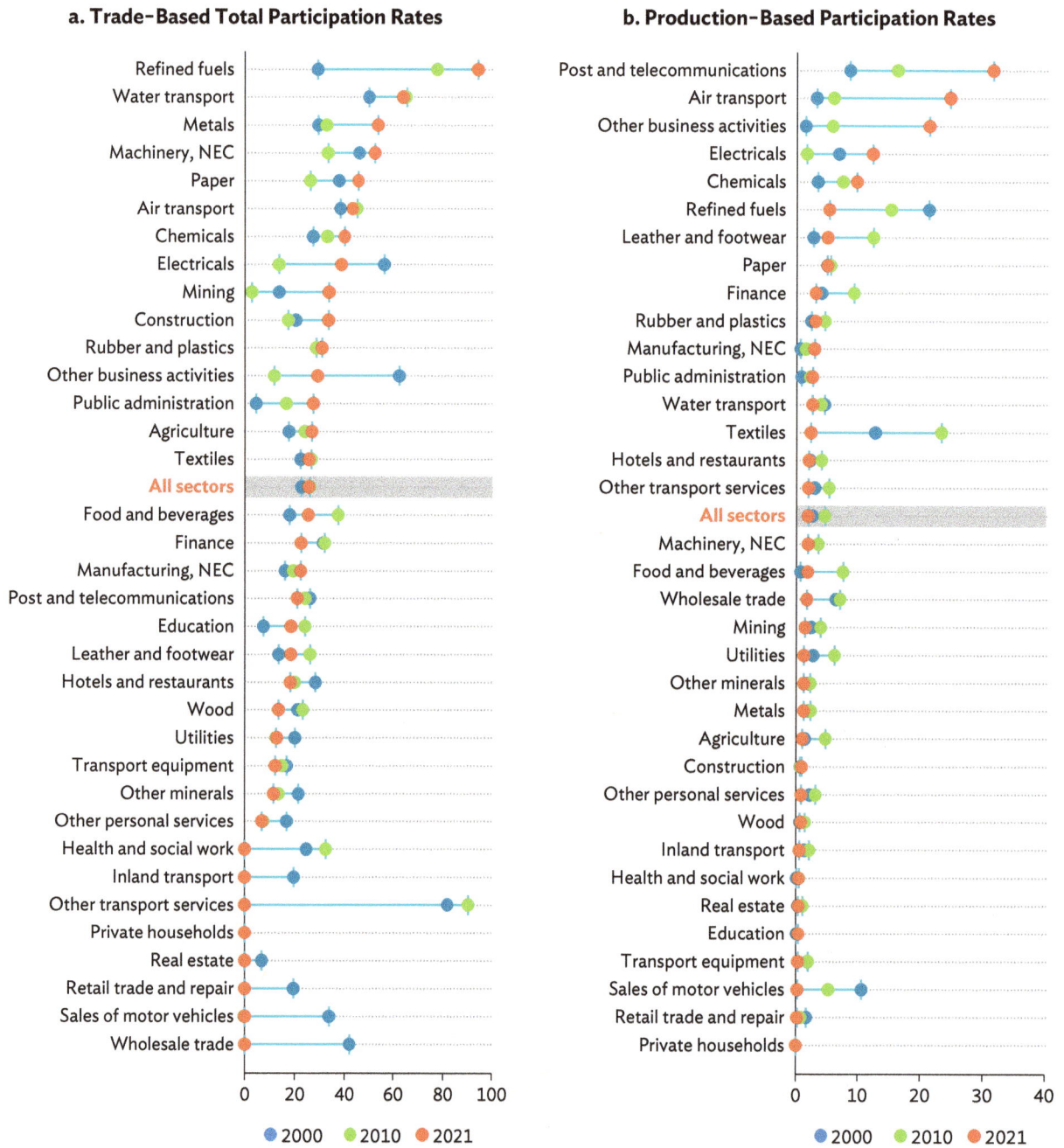

continued on next page.

Figure 3.7 *continued.*

c. Trade–Based Forward Participation Rates

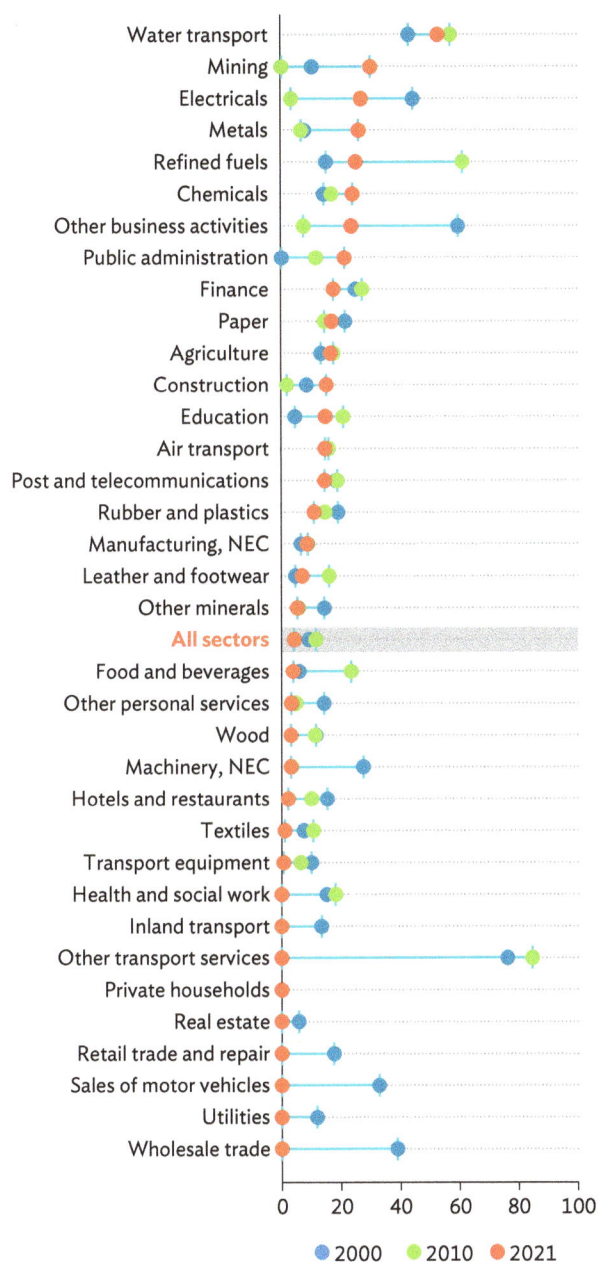

d. Trade–Based Backward Participation Rates

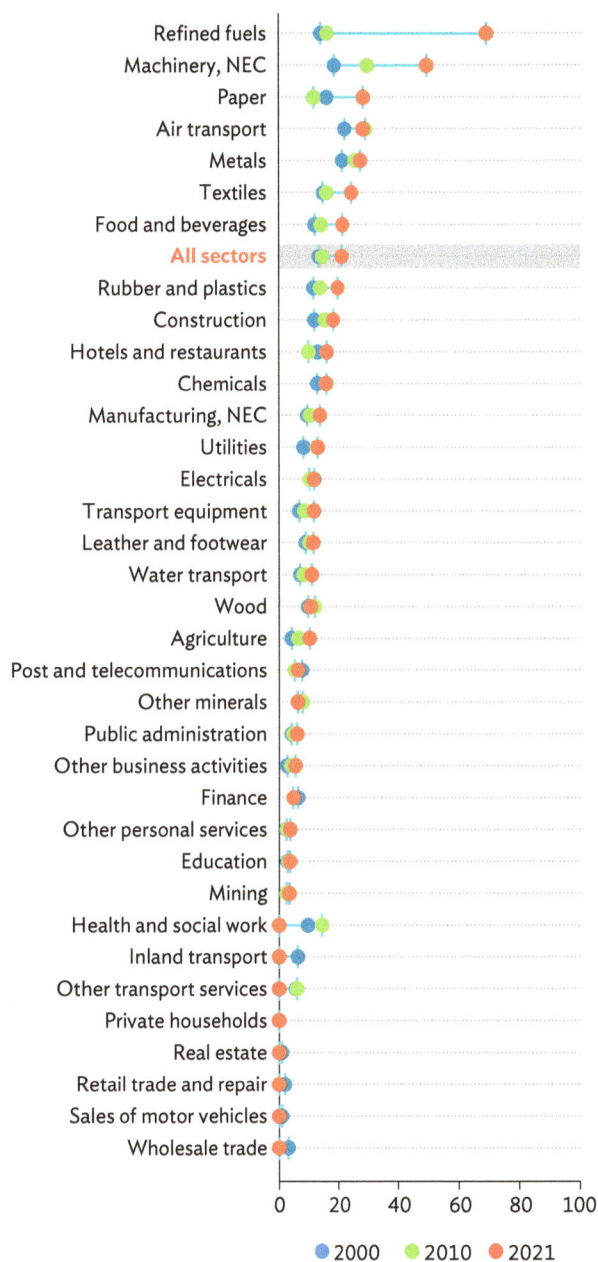

● 2000   ● 2010   ● 2021

NEC = not elsewhere classified.
Notes: Trade-based participation rates are computed using the methodology in Asian Development Bank (2021). The backward participation rate is the share of foreign value-added (FVA) and pure double counting (PDC) in gross exports, while the forward participation rate is the share of domestic value-added exports reexported by the direct importer in gross exports. The production-based participation rate is the share of DAVAX2 (directly absorbed value-added exports by importer as intermediates), REX (reexported by importer and eventually absorbed abroad), and REF (reexported by importer and eventually absorbed by exporter) in gross domestic product. Sector names are shortened according to Appendix 2.
Sources: Asian Development Bank (ADB). 2021. *Key Indicators for Asia and the Pacific 2021*. Manila; ADB. Multiregional Input–Output Database (accessed 14 July 2022); Z. Wang, S. Wei, X. Yu, and K. Zhu. 2017. Measures of Participation in Global Value Chains and Global Business Cycles. *NBER Working Paper*. No. 23222. Cambridge, MA: National Bureau of Economic Research; and ADB estimates.

In the following sector-level participation analysis, the discussion will focus on select sectors with high GVA contributions to GDP or exports. These sectors are (i) agriculture, hunting, forestry, and fishing; (ii) food, beverage, and tobacco; (iii) textiles and textile products; (iv) leather, leather products, and footwear; (v) post and telecommunications; (vi) construction; (vii) renting of machinery and equipment and other business activities; and (viii) public administration and defense; compulsory social security.

The agriculture, hunting, forestry, and fishing sector is Bangladesh's biggest sector in terms of GVA but plays a relatively small role in exports. However, its trade-based GVC participation rate falls slightly above the economy average because of its higher forward participation rates. While its forward participation rate declined from 2010 to 2021, it was offset by an increase in its backward participation rate between the two periods, resulting in an overall increase in GVC participation. For this sector, forward participation plays a larger role than backward participation in GVC. In terms of production-based participation rates, the sector's rates were significantly lower than the economy average and its trade-based forward participation rate. The lower production-based participation rate compared with trade-based forward participation rate is driven by the large portion of GVA that is accounted for by production for domestic consumption.

The food, beverages, and tobacco sector recorded lower than economy-wide total participation rates in 2000 and 2021 but higher than the economy average in 2010. These rates were primarily driven by its forward participation rate rather than its backward participation rate, where data shows that the sector participates in GVCs marginally higher than the economy average. For this sector, forward participation rates were lower than backward participation rates in 2000 and 2021 but higher in 2010.

The textiles and textile products sector is the economy's largest exporting sector and is also among the top GVA sectors. This sector shows lower forward participation compared to backward participation, indicating its high foreign value-added content in exports. Note that this sector is driven by the RMG sector, which is at the more downstream end of the textiles and textiles products GVC chain. Hence, there is already a sizeable foreign value-added embedded in its inputs before Bangladesh processes the product and exports it to destination economies. Additionally, this sector also includes a high portion of value-added in traditional trade, which is why GVC participation may be low. Total participation and forward participation rates for 2021 fell below rates for 2010, following a declining trend since the mid-2010s. On the other hand, backward participation has followed a general upward trend. Comparing the two forward participation indexes also shows that trade-based forward participation falls below production-based participation. This is due to the addition of DAVAX2 or the simple GVCs component in the production-based approach. In the RMG industry, this component plays a significant role as the sector is generally near final consumption in terms of position.

Leather, leather products, and footwear is a closely related sector to the textiles and textile products sector, but its participation rate varies largely from the textiles and textile products sector. The total participation rate for the sector fell below the economy-wide average and the textiles and textile products sector in 2000 and 2021 but was higher in 2010. The trade-based forward participation rate for the sector increased from 2000 to 2010 but declined from 2010 to 2021. Meanwhile, backward participation has increased steadily, albeit only marginally, across the three periods considered.

Bangladesh's construction sector is another large contributor to GDP. In 2021, the sector posted higher trade-based total participation and forward participation rates compared to the economy average. On the other hand, the sector's backward participation rate fell below the economy average. The sector's total participation rate and trade-based forward participation rate in 2000 and 2010 fell below the economy average, while the backward participation rate was above the economy average in 2010. Production-based participation is generally low for the sector because of the large portion of production consumed within Bangladesh in GVA.

Post and telecommunications is the economy's second largest exporting sector. Its trade-based total participation rate fell below the economy aggregate in 2021 but was higher in earlier years. As this is a service-oriented industry, forward participation is naturally higher than backward participation for all years considered. The sector also shows the highest production-based participation rate in 2021, far above the economy-wide average.

Renting of machinery and equipment and other business services is among the top export sectors for Bangladesh. In 2000 and 2021, its total participation rate was higher than the economy average, driven by its large trade-based forward participation rate. On the other hand, 2010 saw a dip in the sector's total participation rate because of the sector's lower-than-average trade-based forward participation rate. The backward participation rate has slightly increased from 2000 to 2010 to 2021. The production-based participation rate for the sector, while lower than trade-based forward participation, has seen an increase from 2000 to 2010 to 2021.

The public administration and defense; compulsory social security sector is consistently among the top contributors to the economy's GDP, but exports from this sector are generally low. Its total GVC participation rate fell above the economy average in 2021 but below the economy average in 2000 and 2010. This higher-than-average total GVC participation for the sector was driven by the relatively higher trade-based forward GVC participation in 2021. Otherwise, both trade-based forward and backward participation fell below the economy average. In terms of production-based participation, the sector also showed the same pattern as in trade-based forward participation, where the rate was only higher than the economy average in 2021. In other years, production-based participation was lower than the economy average. The pattern seen for the sector is also driven by the nature of the activities performed within that sector. The public administration and defense; compulsory social security sector is a service sector than generally caters to the domestic economy, with little to no exports.

C.   Global Value Chain Length and Position

The preceding discussion alluded to a sector or economy's position in GVCs. This position can be measured by first thinking of value chains as a sequence of value-adding steps to create a finished product. Wang et al. (2017a) define the average production length of GVCs as the average number of steps separating domestic value-added creation in intermediate products to its final consumption. On the other hand, they define the backward average production length of GVCs as the average number of steps between the first use of foreign value-added in intermediates as primary inputs until their final absorption into final products. In Wang et al. (2017a), the position of an economy or economy-sector in GVCs can be derived by taking the ratio of forward production length to backward production length. A ratio greater than one implies that an entity is relatively more upstream, while a ratio less than one means an entity is relatively more downstream.

Average production lengths for GVCs in Bangladesh for 2000, 2010, and 2021 are mapped and compared in Figure 3.8. Panel A shows that Bangladesh's forward average GVC length was 4.10 stages in 2000 but lengthened to almost 4.15 in 2010 and 4.17 in 2021. This implies that, at the aggregate level, the value-added created by Bangladesh had to go through increasingly more steps before reaching final use. Meanwhile, changes across sectors vary. Generally, many manufacturing sectors saw declines in forward GVC lengths from 2010 to 2021. However, many other sectors also saw increasing forward GVC lengths in the same period. For the agriculture, hunting, forestry, and fishing sector, the forward average GVC length declined from 4.01 to 3.97 stages between 2000 and 2010 but increased to 4.14 from 2010 to 2021. For the food, beverages, and tobacco sector, the average forward GVC length declined from 4.24 stages in 2000 to 3.12 in 2010 to 3.02 in 2021. Textiles and textile products experienced a decline in length from 3.24 stages in 2000 to 3.15 in 2010. However, the GVC production length faced by the sector increased to 3.55 stages in 2021. Leather, leather products, and footwear followed the same pattern of decline between 2000 and 2010, from 3.76 stages to 3.48, then an increase to 3.65 in 2021. The construction sector showed a different pattern of increasing average forward GVC length between 2000 and 2010 and declining forward GVC length between 2010 and 2021. The construction sector's value-added creation underwent an average of 4.72 stages before reaching final use in 2000, 4.78 stages in 2010, and 3.77 in 2021. Post and telecommunications in Bangladesh experienced declining forward GVC production length, from 3.64 stages in 2000, 3.47 in 2010, and 3.29 in 2021. Similarly, renting of machinery and equipment and other business activities also saw a declining trend in its forward GVC length, from 4.80 stages in 2000 to 3.36 in 2010 to 3.42 in 2021. Finally, public administration and defense; compulsory social security also saw declining forward GVC lengths, from 4.50 stages in 2000 to 3.65 in 2010 and 3.64 in 2021.

Figure 3.8 panel B presents movements in backward average production lengths for GVCs. A comparison between 2000 and 2010 shows that most of Bangladesh's sectors saw a lengthening of backward GVC production lengths, with only two sectors experiencing a shortening of backward GVC production lengths. This is consistent with the increasing share of FVA in exports through time. Sector variations are more prominent when comparing 2010 against 2021, but the aggregate backward GVC production length increased in both instances. Thus, at the aggregate level, Bangladesh experienced a lengthening of its backward linkage, with an increase in the number of stages in its upstream production process. A sector-by-sector comparison shows different patterns. The agriculture, hunting, forestry, and fishing sector and the food, beverages, and tobacco sector saw increasing lengths between 2000 and 2010 and almost the same lengths between 2010 and 2021. The textiles and textile products sector; the leather, leather products, and footwear sector; the construction sector; and the public administration and defense; compulsory social work sector saw serially increasing backward GVC production lengths, with the final products of these sectors seeing increasingly more stages in their upstream production processes. Post and telecommunications had an increase in its backward GVC production length between 2000 and 2010 and a modest decline in 2021 from 2010. Meanwhile, the renting of machinery and equipment and other business services sector experienced declining backward GVC production length from 4.17 stages in 2000 to 4.09 in 2010 to 3.94 in 2021.

Figure 3.8: Bangladesh Global Value Chain Production Lengths by Sector, 2000, 2010, and 2021

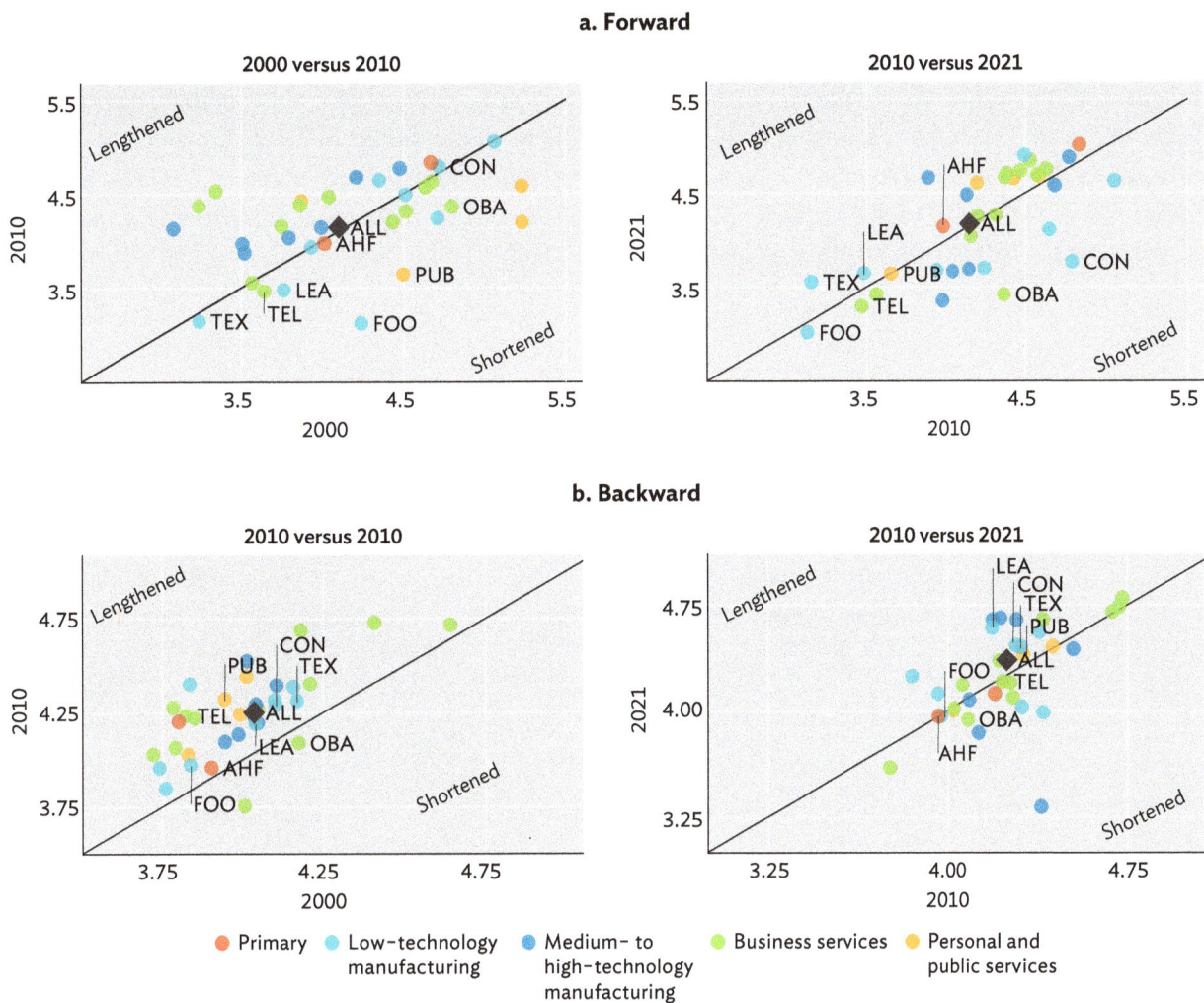

a. Forward

b. Backward

Legend: Primary · Low-technology manufacturing · Medium- to high-technology manufacturing · Business services · Personal and public services

AHF = agriculture, hunting, forestry, and fishing; ALL = all sectors; CON = construction; FOO = food, beverages, and tobacco; LEA = leather, leather products, and footwear; OBA = renting of machinery and equipment and other business activities; PUB = public administration and defense; compulsory social security; TEL = post and telecommunications; TEX = textiles and textile products.

Notes: Average global value chain (GVC) production lengths are computed using the methodology of Wang et al. (2017). Sectors with no GVC production have no lengths and are not included in the chart. Sectors are disaggregated by value-added origins. Color of dots refer to the aggregate sector classification to which a sector belongs.

Sources: Asian Development Bank (ADB). Multiregional Input–Output Database (accessed 14 July 2022); Z. Wang, S. Wei, X. Yu, and K. Zhu. 2017. Characterizing Global Value Chains: Production Length and Upstreamness. *NBER Working Paper*. No. 23261. Cambridge, MA: National Bureau of Economic Research; and ADB estimates.

Wang et al. (2017a) further decomposed production length into two segments—a domestic segment and an international segment. The domestic segment happens before the first border crossing, while the international segment can be broken down into two: (i) border crossing for production and (ii) segment after the first border crossing. Figure 3.9 analyzes these segments for the aggregate economy and select sectors for the forward linkage.

Except for the textiles and textile products sector, all other sectors in Figure 3.9 show that the domestic stages in GVC production lengths declined between 2000 and 2021. For the business services considered in the figure, this decline in domestic stages continued from the decline between 2000 and 2010. On the other hand, for agriculture, food and beverages, leather and footwear, and textiles, there appears to be a reversal in 2021 of the dropped that occurred between 2000 and 2010. For the textiles and textile products sector, this reversal resulted in a higher number of domestic stages in 2021 compared to 2000. Construction follows a different pattern, where domestic length increased in 2010 from 2000 and then declined in 2021. The aggregate economy follows a similar pattern as in construction, where domestic stages increased in 2010 from 2000 and then fell in 2021.

Figure 3.9: Bangladesh Forward Global Value Chain Production Lengths for Selected Sectors, 2000, 2010, and 2021

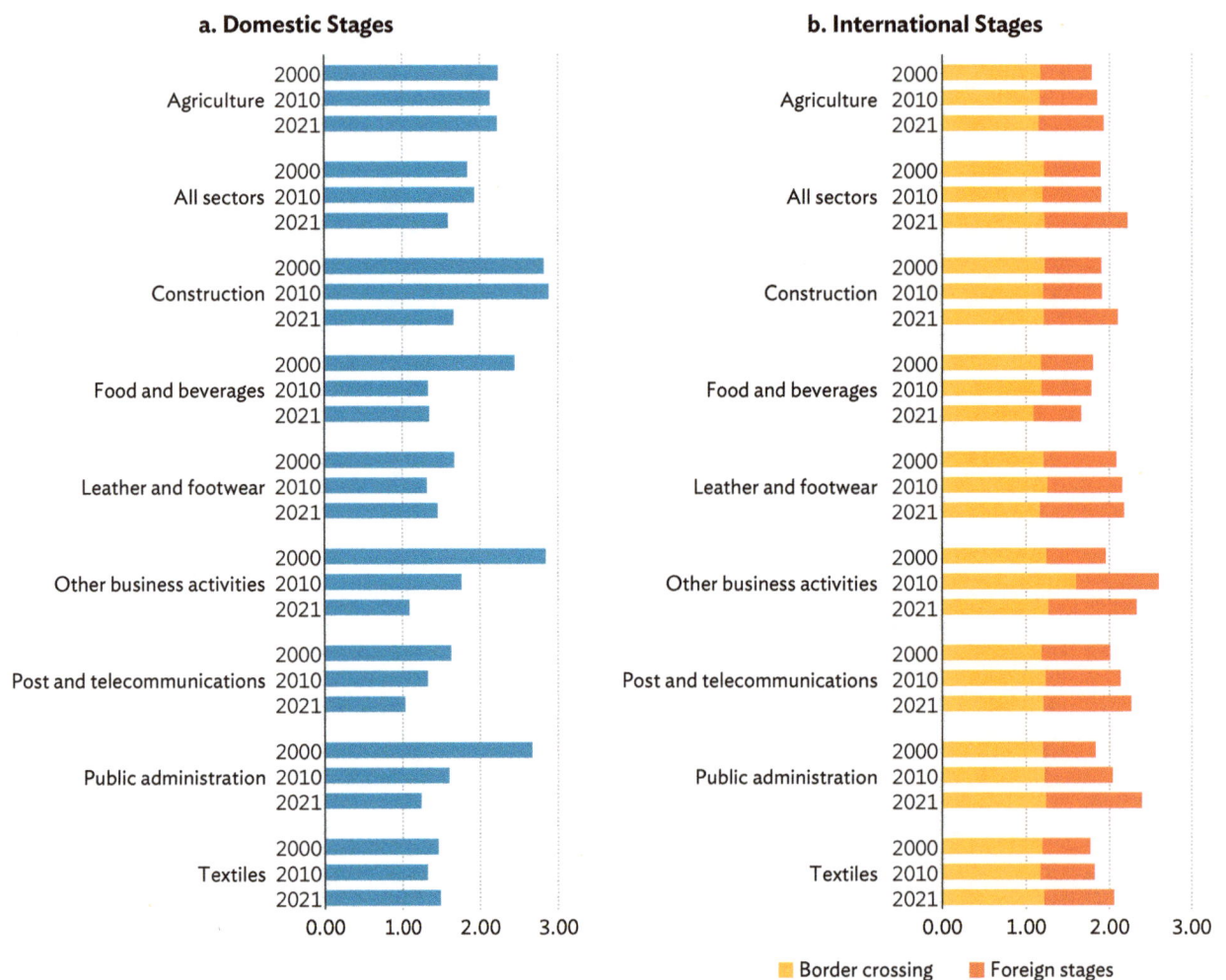

Notes: Average global value chain production lengths are computed using the methodology of Wang et al. (2017). Sectors are disaggregated by value-added origins. Sector names are shortened according to Appendix 2.
Sources: Asian Development Bank (ADB). Multiregional Input–Output Database (accessed 14 July 2022); Z. Wang, S. Wei, X. Yu, and K. Zhu. 2017. Characterizing Global Value Chains: Production Length and Upstreamness. *NBER Working Paper*. No. 23261. Cambridge, MA: National Bureau of Economic Research; and ADB estimates.

In general, the border crossing segment portion of GVC production length makes up over half of all international stages, and their patterns also differ from the production stages that occur in foreign economies. For instance, the GVC production length for the aggregate economy has an almost unchanged number of border crossings between 2000 and 2010, but it saw a decline in this segment between 2010 and 2021. On the other hand, the foreign segment for the aggregate economy increased between 2000 and 2010 but declined between 2010 and 2021. The agriculture sector saw a decrease in the average number of border crossings between 2000 and 2010 and an increase between 2010 and 2021. However, the average number of stages occurring abroad increased and then declined. For the textiles sector, the number of border crossings declined between 2000 and 2010 and increased between 2010 and 2021. Meanwhile, the average number of production stages occurring abroad increased from 2000 to 2010 to 2021.

Figure 3.10 and Figure 3.11 take the ratio of the forward and backward average GVC production lengths to give the GVC positions of all economies in the ADB-MRIOTs.[3] Bangladesh's position in GVCs relative to other economies is depicted in Figure 3.10. First, Bangladesh falls relatively downstream across all years compared to the world average GVC position. Second, compared to competitors, Bangladesh was relatively upstream until 2013. From 2014 onwards, except in 2015, Bangladesh has moved downstream and is only more upstream than Cambodia for most years.

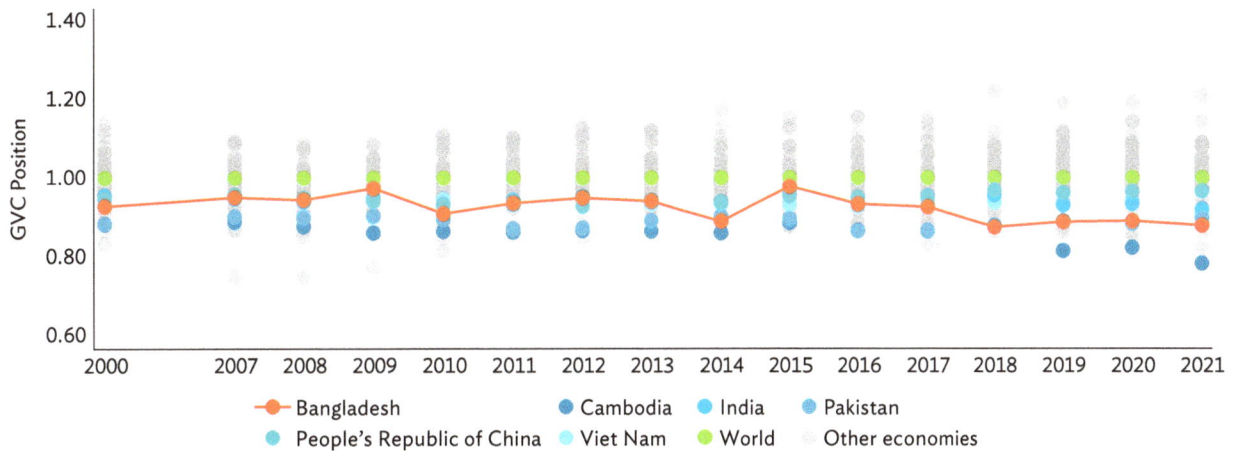

Figure 3.10: Global Value Chain Position of 62 Economies and the Rest of the World, 2000, 2007–2021

GVC = global value chain.
Note: Average GVC positions are computed using the methodology of Wang et al. (2017).
Sources: Asian Development Bank (ADB). Multiregional Input–Output Database (accessed 14 July 2022); Z. Wang, S. Wei, X. Yu, and K. Zhu. 2017. Characterizing Global Value Chains: Production Length and Upstreamness. *NBER Working Paper*. No. 23261. Cambridge, MA: National Bureau of Economic Research; and ADB estimates.

---

[3]   As Wang et al. (2017a) point out, this index can be different from positions when taking total production lengths, as total production lengths would concern an economy's or economy-sector's production as a whole, where pure domestic production activities are significant.

Figure 3.11: Global Value Chain Position in the Textiles and Textile Products Sector of 62 Economies and the Rest of the World, 2000, 2007–2021

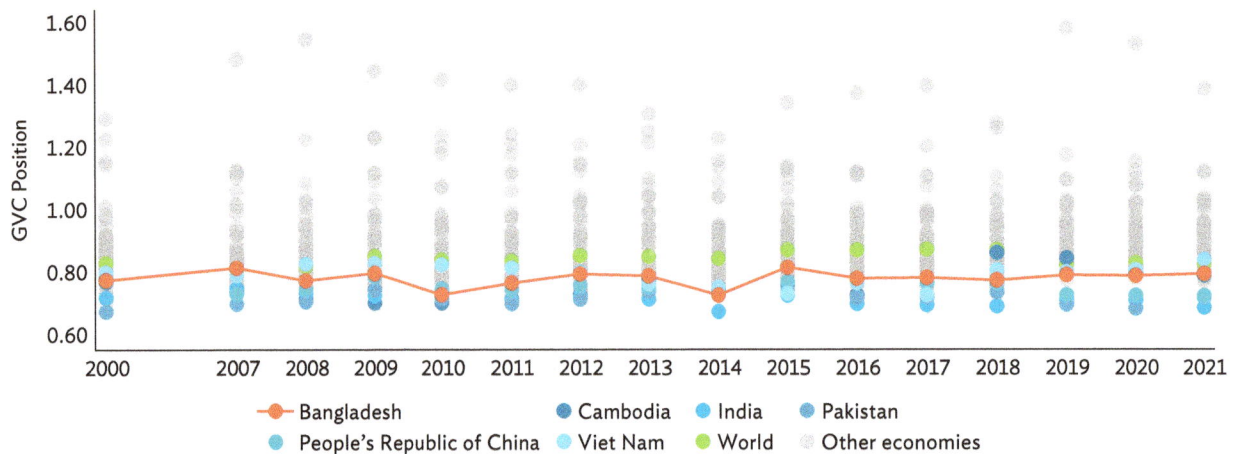

GVC = global value chain.
Note: Average GVC positions are computed using the methodology of Wang et al. (2017).
Sources: Asian Development Bank (ADB). Multiregional Input–Output Database (accessed 14 July 2022); Z. Wang, S. Wei, X. Yu, and K. Zhu. 2017. Characterizing Global Value Chains: Production Length and Upstreamness. *NBER Working Paper*. No. 23261. Cambridge, MA: National Bureau of Economic Research; and ADB estimates.

Within the textiles and textile products sector, as in Figure 3.11, Bangladesh's relative position compared to the world average is generally more downstream, except in 2007. However, beginning in 2019, Bangladesh's position in the GVCs for the textiles and textile products sector is converging with the world average for two reasons. First, Bangladesh has very slightly moved upstream from its level in 2018. Second, the world average has moved downstream from its level in 2018. Compared to several of its competitors, Bangladesh is relatively more upstream in the GVCs for textiles and textile products, especially in earlier years. Beginning 2019, however, some of its competitors appear to have moved relatively more upstream, with some becoming more upstream than Bangladesh.

Using arrows, Figure 3.12 indicates whether sectors in Bangladesh have moved upstream or downstream within GVCs between 2000 and 2010 and between 2010 and 2021. Data shows that, at the aggregate level, Bangladesh moved slightly downstream from 2000 to 2010 to 2021. This was mainly driven by a more significant lengthening of its backward GVC production length compared with its forward GVC production length. Meanwhile, many economy-sectors in Bangladesh moved downstream or closer to final consumption between 2000 and 2010. On the other hand, half of Bangladesh's economy-sectors moved upstream, while the other half moved downstream between 2010 and 2021.

For instance, the agriculture sector and the textiles sector moved downstream between 2000 and 2010 and then upstream between 2010 and 2021. Between 2000 and 2010, the forward GVC production length declined, while the backward GVC production length increased for the agriculture sector and the textiles sector, leading to their movement downstream. For these two sectors, the increases in their forward GVC production length between 2010 and 2021 were larger than the increases in their backward GVC production length, leading to their overall movement upstream between the two periods.

Figure 3.12: Bangladesh Global Value Chain Position by Sector

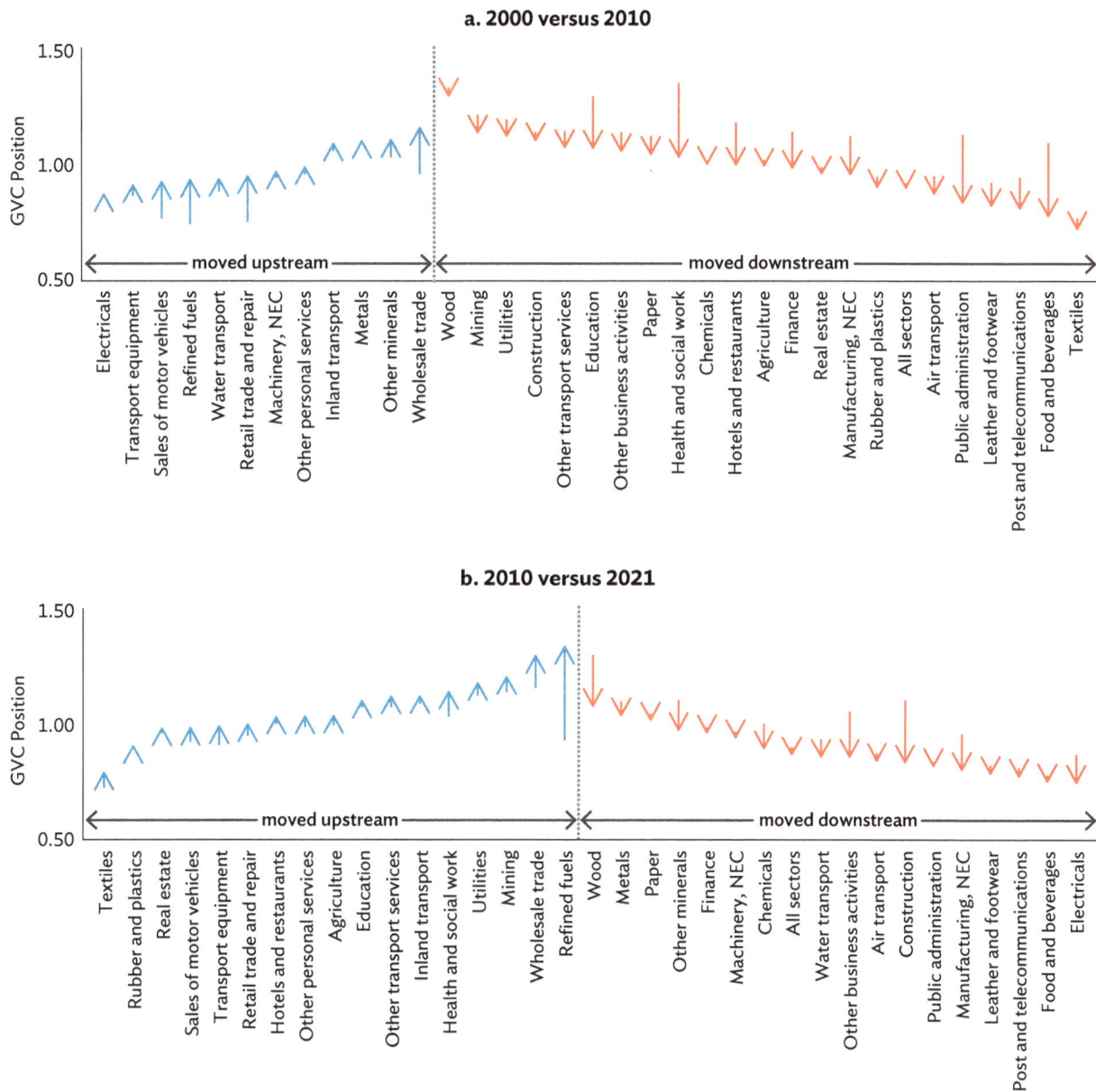

a. 2000 versus 2010

b. 2010 versus 2021

GVC = global value chain, NEC = not elsewhere classified.

Notes: Average GVC positions are computed using the methodology of Wang et al. (2017). Arrowhead tips represent GVC positions in the second period, while arrow-line ends represent values for the first period. Sectors are disaggregated by value-added origins. Sector names are shortened according to Appendix 2.

Sources: Asian Development Bank (ADB). Multiregional Input–Output Database (accessed 14 July 2022); Z. Wang, S. Wei, X. Yu, and K. Zhu. 2017. Characterizing Global Value Chains: Production Length and Upstreamness. NBER Working Paper. No. 23261. Cambridge, MA: National Bureau of Economic Research; and ADB estimates.

The food and beverages sector, the leather sector, the construction sector, the post and telecommunications sector, the other business activities sector, and the public administration sector moved closer to final consumption from 2000 to 2010 to 2021. A closer look at the changes in forward and backward GVC production lengths can explain the declines experienced by these sectors between 2000 and 2010, and between 2010 and 2021.

The food and beverages sector saw a significant decline in its forward GVC production length and a decline in its backward GVC production length between 2000 and 2010. The leather and footwear sector also saw a decrease in its forward GVC production length and an increase in its backward production length from 2000 to 2010. While the construction sector saw increases in both its forward and backward GVC production lengths, the increase was relatively more significant in its backward linkage, leading to a movement downstream between 2000 and 2010. The post and telecommunications sector saw a decline in its forward GVC production length and an increase in its backward GVC production length between 2000 and 2010. The other business activities sector saw a decline in both its forward and backward GVC production lengths between 2000 and 2010, with a more significant decrease in its forward GVC production length. Finally, the public administration sector experienced a substantial shortening of its forward GVC production length and an increase in its backward GVC production length from 2000 to 2010.

Between 2010 and 2021, the food and beverages sector experienced a larger decline in its forward GVC production length than its backward GVC production length. The leather and footwear sector saw an increase in its forward GVC production length between 2010 and 2021, but it saw an even greater increase in its backward GVC production length, ending in an overall movement downstream. The construction sector was among the sectors that saw a significant movement downstream between 2010 and 2021 because of a decline of more than one stage in its forward GVC production length and a mild increase in its backward GVC production length. Between 2010 and 2021, the post and telecommunications sector saw a more significant shortening of its forward GVC production length versus its backward GVC production length. As with the construction sector, the other business activities sector also saw a large decline in its forward GVC production length and only a slight decline in its backward GVC production length between 2010 and 2021. On the other hand, the public administration sector saw a mild decline in its forward GVC production length and a larger increase in its backward GVC production length between 2010 and 2021.

In summary, GVC data shows that Bangladesh's export comprises a large portion of domestic value-added involved in traditional trade rather than GVCs. This can be explained by Bangladesh's concentration in the textiles and textile products sector for exports. Bangladesh's textiles and textile products mainly involve RMG, a finished or near-finished good. While the sector's backward GVC participation may be significant when considering only GVC-related value-added, its FVA share is dwarfed by the magnitude of DAVAX in its gross exports.

Considering GVCs alone, Bangladesh has higher backward participation than forward participation, as implied by its larger share of FVA relative to its forward components, REX and REF. The trends and patterns in participation rates would suggest that Bangladesh is located downstream within GVC chains. Additionally, a more formal measure of GVC position following Wang et al. (2017a) shows that Bangladesh has moved further downstream over the years with a lengthening of its backward GVC production length, although patterns differ across sectors.

Chapter 4
DIVERSIFICATION, SPECIALIZATION, AND AGGLOMERATION

The last two preceding chapters discussed the significant dominance of the textiles and textile products sector in Bangladesh's exports. In Chapter 2, the Herfindahl–Hirschman Index (HHI), which is computed using product exports, showed that Bangladesh is the most concentrated economy against its competitors in textile products. Chapter 3 also showed that the textiles and textile products sector forms a large part of exports and value-added components of exports. Such dominance drives the economy's relatively low aggregate global value chain (GVC) participation rates.

This chapter aims to reveal some aspects of the interconnectedness of production activities within the domestic economy despite the significant concentration of export products in textiles. Exports usually carry a portion of value-added that originates from the domestic economy and another portion that originates from foreign economies. Under a gross exports approach and an exporting-sector view, these contributions of other domestic sectors are not counted as exports of these originating sectors. To correctly assign these indirect exports to origin sectors, an origin sector or forward approach to decomposition is necessary. Additionally, considering only domestic value-added takes away the contribution of foreign value-added in exports.

Under this premise, this chapter continues the discussion of the economy's level of diversification using sector-level data. It employs the methodology proposed by Bajaj et al. (2022) in comparing two HHIs—one using gross exports and one using value-added exports. A value-added exports approach to computing for diversification brings out the contribution of the other sectors in exports that may not be captured by traditional measures of diversification, which use only gross exports. As with diversification, this chapter will also use forward value-added exports and gross exports to assess Bangladesh's sector specialization. The primary measure used to explore specialization will be the revealed comparative advantage (RCA) index, as in Balassa (1965), but modified for value-added exports. The Balassa RCA index will also be normalized using Yu, Cai, and Leung (2009) to make it comparable across sectors, economies, and time. Finally, this chapter will tackle agglomeration in Bangladesh and compare it with other economies. The main indicators for agglomeration are derived from the work of Mercer-Blackman, Foronda, and Mariasingham (2017), as refined by Baris et al. (2022).

An important indicator for computing value-added-based HHIs and RCA is what Wang et al. (2017b) term VAX_F. In the Borin and Mancini (2019) framework, this is equivalent to the sum of domestic value-added directly absorbed by the importer (DAVAX) and domestic value-added reexported by the importer and eventually absorbed by the exporter (REF) when exports are decomposed by origin sector. These two components are accessible through the ADB GVC indicators database and are used here to compute the HHIs and RCA indexes.[4]

---

4   ADB. Multiregional Input–Output Database. http://mrio.adbx.online.

A.   Diversification

HHI is calculated by taking the square of each sector's share in an economy's exports and then summing these squares up. To make HHIs comparable across economies and across time, this computed HHI is normalized by subtracting one over the number of active sectors in the economy from the sum of squared shares and then dividing this by one minus one over the number of active sectors in the economy, as follows:

$$HHI = \frac{\sum_{n=1}^{E} (S_i^r)^2 - \frac{1}{N}}{1 - 1/N}$$

where S_i^r is the share of gross exports or value-added exports of sector i in economy r, and N is the number of active sectors in economy r. This normalized HHI ensures that the values of the index range between 0 and 1. A value of 1 implies that an economy is highly specialized and exports through just one sector. A value of 0 means that each sector shares equally in exports or value-added exports and the economy is homogenously diversified. Thus, the higher the HHI, the more concentrated an economy.

Figure 4.1 compares Bangladesh's level of diversification against its competitors for 2000 and 2007–2021. Several observations can be made. First, comparing the two charts (panels A and B) shows that Bangladesh's HHI using gross exports is significantly higher than its HHI using value-added exports. This suggests that the sectors contributing to exports, whether directly or indirectly, are more diverse than exporting sectors. Thus, the role of other domestic sectors is important in supporting the export production of the major direct exporting sectors, such as textiles and textile products.

Second, Bangladesh is more diverse today than at the beginning of the millennium, but there have been alternate periods of increasing concentration and diversification from 2000 to 2021. Both panels A and B show that diversification in Bangladesh initially increased from 2000 until 2008. However, beginning in 2009, there was a pattern of growing concentration until 2016 for gross exports and 2018 for value-added exports, followed by increasing diversification until 2021.

Third, panel A shows that Bangladesh has the highest concentration using gross exports among competitors and is significantly more specialized than its competitors. However, diversification when using value-added exports (panel B) shows that it is more on par with Cambodia and Pakistan. Panel B also shows that in 2007–2012, Cambodia had a more concentrated export production activity compared with Bangladesh. In 2013, however, Bangladesh's HHI exceeded Cambodia, as Bangladesh's HHIs increased while Cambodia's declined. Their positions reversed again during the COVID-19 pandemic in 2020 and 2021, with Bangladesh increasing its diversification since 2019 and Cambodia increasing its concentration after a trough in 2019.

Figure 4.1: Herfindahl–Hirschman Indexes of Selected Economies Using Sector Exports, 2000, 2007–2021

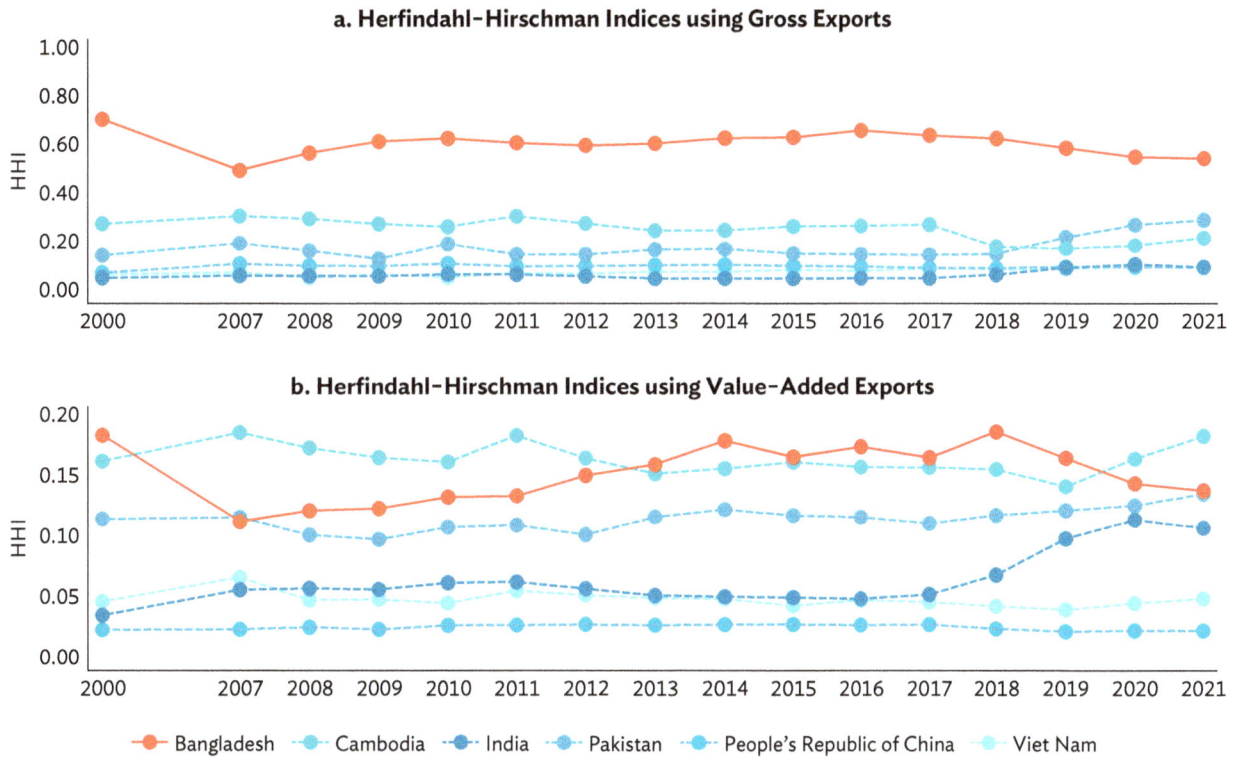

a. Herfindahl-Hirschman Indices using Gross Exports

b. Herfindahl-Hirschman Indices using Value-Added Exports

Bangladesh — Cambodia — India — Pakistan — People's Republic of China — Viet Nam

HHI = Herfindahl-Hirschman Index.

Notes: HHI measures an economy's export diversification. A higher HHI indicates a lower level of diversification. HHI using value-added exports is computed using the sum of DAVAX and REX from an origin sector decomposition. DAVAX are directly absorbed domestic value-added exports, while REX are domestic value-added exports reexported by direct importer and eventually absorbed abroad.

Sources: Asian Development Bank (ADB). 2021. *Key Indicators for Asia and the Pacific 2021*. Manila; ADB. Multiregional Input–Output Database (accessed 14 July 2022); and ADB estimates.

The shares of sectors can explain the patterns of the two HHIs in total gross exports and DAVAX plus domestic value-added directly absorbed by the imported and eventually absorbed abroad (REX) (Figure 4.2). The significantly higher percentage of the textiles and textile products sector in gross exports (panel A) accounts for the much larger HHI based on gross exports compared with HHI based on value-added. Panel B shows that while the textiles and textile products sector still comprises a large share of value-added exports, sector shares are relatively more balanced. Data on DAVAX and REX reveal that sectors like agriculture, wholesale trade, post and telecommunications, finance, other business services, and other personal services also play large, albeit indirect, roles in exports. Additionally, the share of the textiles and textile products sector only reaches 32%–42% when looking at value-added exports, in contrast to 71%–85% when looking at gross exports. Hence, HHI based on value-added exports will be lower.

Changes in the HHIs are also directly related to the changes in shares of sectors. The changes in the sector shares, especially in the textiles and textile products sector, drive the trends in HHI. In the years when the share of the textiles and textile products in total gross and value-added exports decreased, Bangladesh also experienced an increase in diversification from both perspectives. However, in terms of value-added, the other sectors also have a more significant influence on HHI.

Figure 4.2: Bangladesh Share of Sectors in Gross Exports and DAVAX + REX, 2000, 2007–2021

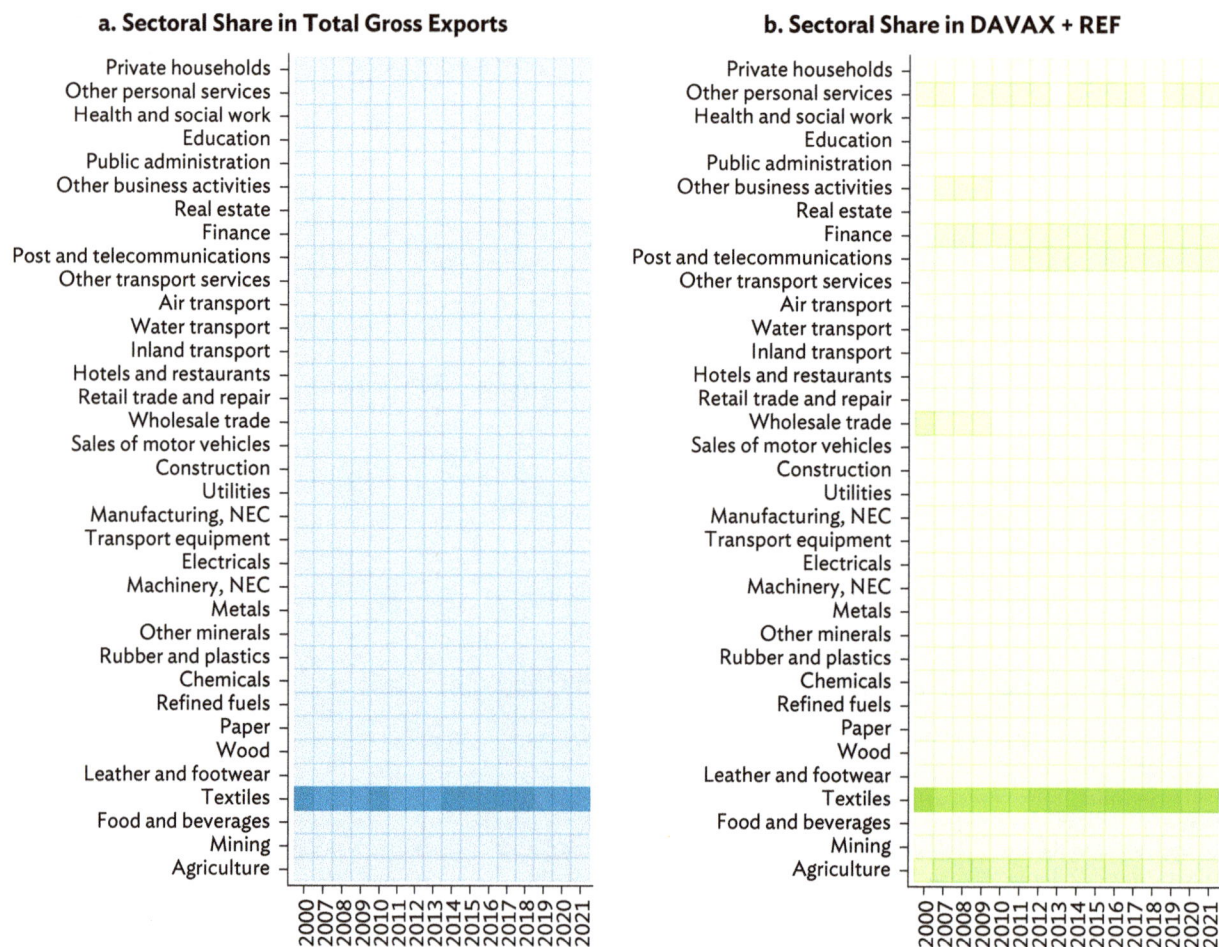

a. Sectoral Share in Total Gross Exports

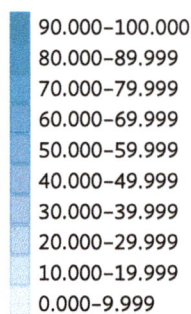

b. Sectoral Share in DAVAX + REF

Share in Total Gross Exports (%)

	90.000–100.000
	80.000–89.999
	70.000–79.999
	60.000–69.999
	50.000–59.999
	40.000–49.999
	30.000–39.999
	20.000–29.999
	10.000–19.999
	0.000–9.999

Share in Total DAVAX + REF (%)

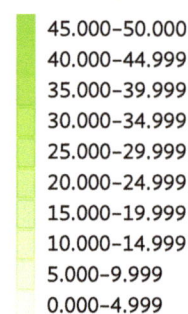

	45.000–50.000
	40.000–44.999
	35.000–39.999
	30.000–34.999
	25.000–29.999
	20.000–24.999
	15.000–19.999
	10.000–14.999
	5.000–9.999
	0.000–4.999

NEC = not elsewhere classified.
Notes: DAVAX are directly absorbed value-added exports, while REX are domestic value-added exports reexported by direct importer and eventually absorbed abroad. DAVAX and REX are from an origin sector decomposition of exports. Sector names are shortened according to Appendix 2.
Sources: Asian Development Bank (ADB). 2021. *Key Indicators for Asia and the Pacific 2021*. Manila; ADB. Multiregional Input–Output Database (accessed 14 July 2022); and ADB estimates.

B.   Specialization and Competitiveness

Another indicator where a value-added exports approach is useful is RCA, which is used to indicate an economy's specialization or competitiveness. The RCA index is a relative measure in that it compares an economy-sector's share in total economy exports to the share of that sector in world exports. Alternatively, it compares the share of economy r's sector i in total world exports of sector i to economy r's share in total world exports. Based on Balassa (1965), the RCA of sector i in economy r is given by the following equation:

$$BRCA_{i,r} = \frac{E_i^r/E^r}{E_i/E} \text{ or } BRCA_{i,r} = \frac{E_r^i/E_i}{E^r/E}$$

where $BRCA_{i,r}$ is the Balassa (1965) revealed comparative advantage index of economy r sector i, E_i^r is the exports of sector i in economy r, E^r is the total exports of economy r, E_i is the sum of sector i exports across all economies in the world, and E is total world exports. Economy r is said to have comparative advantage in sector i whenever $RCA_{i,r} > 1$ and comparative disadvantage whenever $RCA_{i,r} < 1$. Whenever $RCA_{i,r} = 1$, economy r is considered to have neutral comparative advantage in that sector.

To make the RCA comparable across sectors, economies, and time, Yu, Cai, and Leung (2009) proposed a normalization of the Balassa (1965) RCA as follows:

$$NRCA_{i,r} = \frac{E_i^r}{E} - \frac{E_i/E^r}{E\,E}$$

where $NRCA_{i,r}$ is the normalized RCA index of economy r sector i, E_i^r is the exports of sector i in economy r, E^r is the total exports of economy r, E^r is the sum of sector i exports across all economies in the world, and E is total world exports. Unlike in the Balassa (1965) index, economy r is said to have comparative advantage in sector i whenever $NRCA_{i,r} > 0$ and comparative disadvantage whenever $NRCA_{i,r} < 0$. Whenever $RCA_{i,r} = 0$, economy r is considered to have neutral comparative advantage in that sector. According to Yu, Cai, and Leung (2009), this normalized RCA index measures the degree of deviation of an economy's actual exports from its neutral comparative advantage level in terms of its relative scale with respect to world exports. This allows for a comparison among entities with different normalized revealed comparative advantage (NRCA) indexes. For instance, if the NRCA of economy r sector 1 is higher than its NRCA in sector 2, then economy r has a stronger comparative advantage in sector 1 than in sector 2. Another example is a comparison of NRCA indexes between two economies exporting in the same sector. An economy with a higher NRCA, given that both have NRCA > 0, would have a stronger comparative advantage in that sector. Finally, when the NRCA of an economy in a sector grows over time, such that NRCA in time 1 is larger than NRCA in time 2, the economy is said to have increased its comparative advantage in that sector.

Yu, Cai, and Leung (2009) prove that NRCA indexes range from –0.25 to 0.25, with 0 being the neutral comparative advantage. NRCA indexes were multiplied by 10,000 in this report for analysis and presentation purposes. This does not change the analysis given the range and distribution of the NRCA.

Figure 4.3 shows and compares NRCA using gross exports and NRCA using value-added exports in Bangladesh for 2021. Based on these two approaches, Bangladesh has revealed comparative advantage in six sectors: (i) textiles and textile products; (ii) post and telecommunications; (iii) leather, leather products, and footwear; (iv) public administration and defense; compulsory social work; (v) construction; and (vi) manufacturing, not elsewhere classified (NEC). Additional five sectors also have revealed comparative advantage when using a value-added exports approach because of the indirect contribution of these sectors to the exports of the other sectors and the removal of foreign value-added when using the value-added exports approach. These sectors include (i) agriculture, hunting, forestry, and fishing; (ii) other community, social, and personal services sector; (iii) finance; (iv) other nonmetallic minerals; and (v) inland transport.

NRCA indexes for 2021 show that Bangladesh has the strongest RCA in the textiles and textile products sector regardless of approach. However, the textiles sector's RCA index weakens from 11.8 under the gross exports approach to 6.4 under the value-added approach. For the post and telecommunications sector, the NRCA index went down from 0.9 in the gross exports approach to 0.8 in the value-added exports approach. The NRCA indexes for these two sectors show that Bangladesh's comparative advantage in the textiles and textile products sector is at least eight times larger than its comparative advantage in the next biggest exporting sector, post and telecommunications.

For the leather, leather products, and footwear sector x, the RCA index was at 4.6 in the gross exports approach but was at 6.2 in the value-added exports approach. The sector shows a very different ranking under a gross exports approach and a value-added exports approach. It ranked third in the gross exports approach but only sixth under a value-added exports approach. Again, this is in part because of the indirect contribution of the other sectors, like the agriculture, hunting, forestry, and fishing sector and the other community, social, and personal services sector, where Bangladesh has comparative disadvantage under a gross exports approach and comparative advantage under a value-added exports approach.

Bangladesh regained comparative advantage in the construction sector using the gross exports approach only beginning in 2019 after losing its advantage in 2009. However, NRCA based on value-added exports shows that the sector has consistently been a comparative advantage sector for Bangladesh since 2000. Meanwhile, Bangladesh only gained comparative advantage in the manufacturing, NEC; recycling sector in 2020 under the value-added exports approach and in 2021 under the gross exports approach.

More details on the evolution of RCA in Bangladesh are presented in Figure 4.4. (page 36 to 37). Panel A shows the time series of RCA for primary sectors, panel B shows those for low-technology manufacturing sectors, panel C shows those for medium- to high-technology sectors, panel D shows those for business services sectors, and panel E shows those for the personal and public services sector.

Figure 4.4.a shows that under a gross exports approach, Bangladesh had RCA in the agriculture, hunting, forestry, and fishing sector in 2000 and 2007 but lost its comparative advantage in this sector beginning in 2008. Additionally, its comparative disadvantage in the sector is growing stronger, as indicated by the declining trend in NRCA. On the other hand, the sector is an RCA sector for Bangladesh when looking at the value-added approach. Under this approach, the economy strengthened its comparative advantage in this sector from the early 2000s to the mid-2010s, but it has shown a weakening advantage since 2017.

Figure 4.3: Normalized Revealed Comparative Advantage of Sectors, Bangladesh, 2021

a. NRCA based on Gross Exports

b. NRCA based on Value-Added Exports

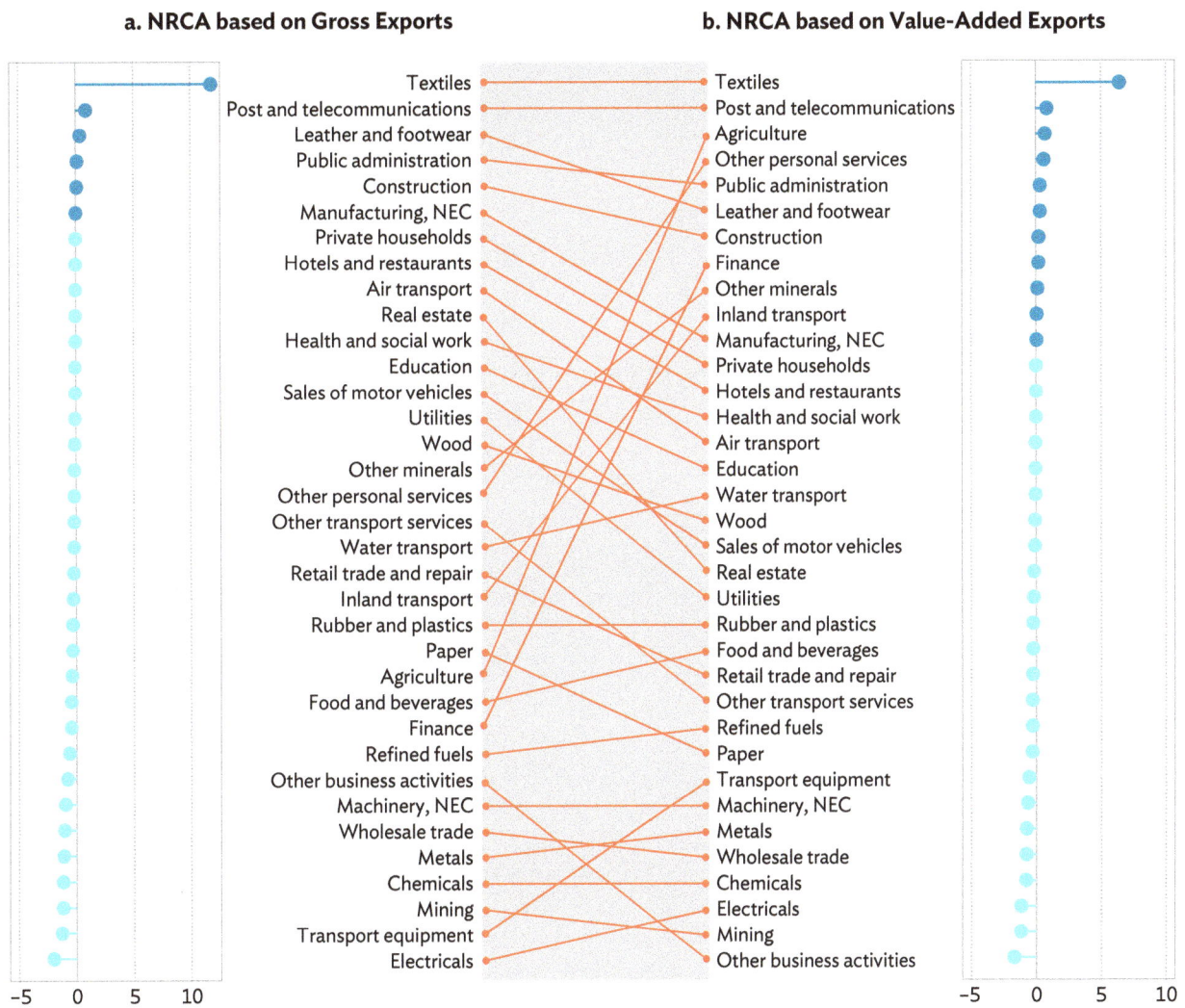

a. NRCA based on Gross Exports	b. NRCA based on Value-Added Exports
Textiles	Textiles
Post and telecommunications	Post and telecommunications
Leather and footwear	Agriculture
Public administration	Other personal services
Construction	Public administration
Manufacturing, NEC	Leather and footwear
Private households	Construction
Hotels and restaurants	Finance
Air transport	Other minerals
Real estate	Inland transport
Health and social work	Manufacturing, NEC
Education	Private households
Sales of motor vehicles	Hotels and restaurants
Utilities	Health and social work
Wood	Air transport
Other minerals	Education
Other personal services	Water transport
Other transport services	Wood
Water transport	Sales of motor vehicles
Retail trade and repair	Real estate
Inland transport	Utilities
Rubber and plastics	Rubber and plastics
Paper	Food and beverages
Agriculture	Retail trade and repair
Food and beverages	Other transport services
Finance	Refined fuels
Refined fuels	Paper
Other business activities	Transport equipment
Machinery, NEC	Machinery, NEC
Wholesale trade	Metals
Metals	Wholesale trade
Chemicals	Chemicals
Mining	Electricals
Transport equipment	Mining
Electricals	Other business activities

NEC = not elsewhere classified, NRCA = normalized revealed comparative advantage.
Notes: NRCA indexes are computed according to Balassa (1965) and Yu, Cai, and Leung (2009) and multiplied by 10,000. Value-added exports are computed by summing DAVAX and REX from an origin sector decomposition of exports. DAVAX are directly absorbed value-added exports, while REX are domestic value-added exports reexported by direct importer and eventually absorbed abroad. Sectors with revealed comparative advantage are highlighted in blue and boldface letters. Sector names are shortened according to Appendix 2.
Sources: Asian Development Bank (ADB). 2021. *Key Indicators for Asia and the Pacific 2021*. Manila; ADB. Multiregional Input–Output Database (accessed 14 July 2022); B. Balassa. 1965. Trade Liberalisation and "Revealed" Comparative Advantage. *The Manchester School*. 33 (2). pp. 99–123; R. Yu, J. Cai, and P. S. Leung. 2009. The Normalized Revealed Comparative Advantage Index. *Annals of Regional Science*. 43 (1). pp. 267–282; and ADB estimates.

Figure 4.4: Normalized Revealed Comparative Advantage, Bangladesh

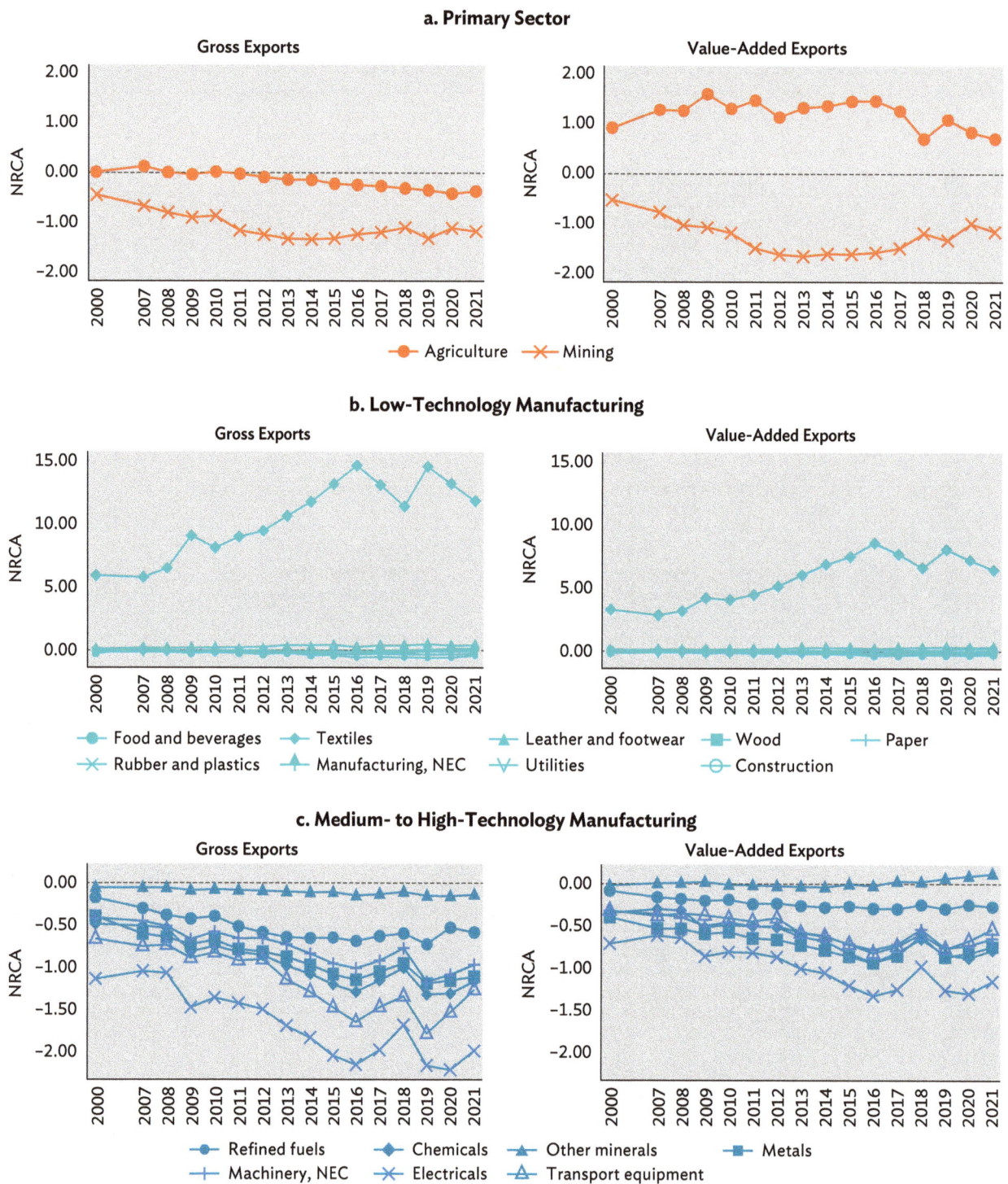

a. Primary Sector

Gross Exports | Value-Added Exports

Agriculture — Mining

b. Low-Technology Manufacturing

Gross Exports | Value-Added Exports

Food and beverages — Textiles — Leather and footwear — Wood — Paper — Rubber and plastics — Manufacturing, NEC — Utilities — Construction

c. Medium- to High-Technology Manufacturing

Gross Exports | Value-Added Exports

Refined fuels — Chemicals — Other minerals — Metals — Machinery, NEC — Electricals — Transport equipment

continued on next page.

Figure 4.4 *continued.*

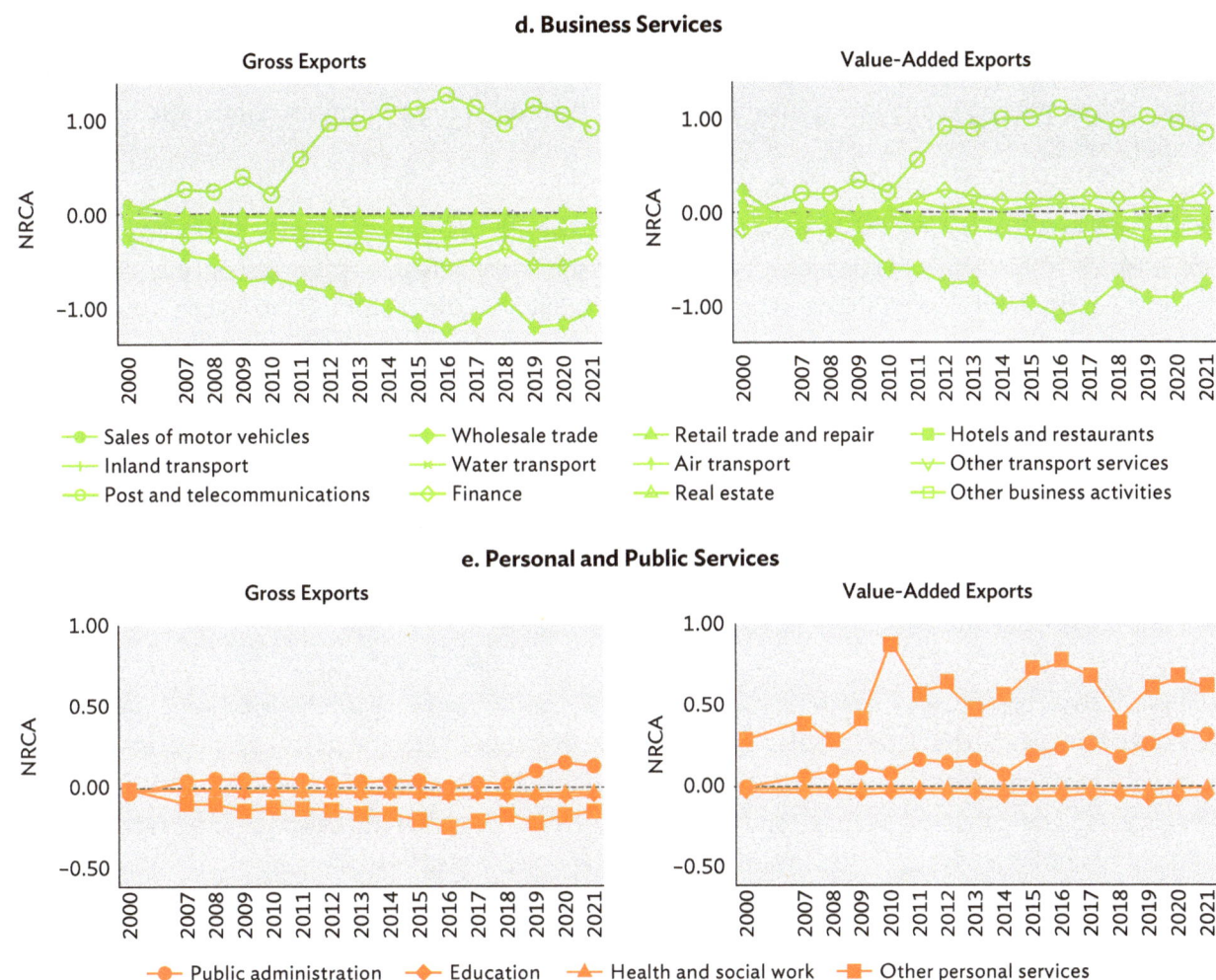

d. Business Services

Gross Exports

Value-Added Exports

Legend:
- Sales of motor vehicles
- Wholesale trade
- Retail trade and repair
- Hotels and restaurants
- Inland transport
- Water transport
- Air transport
- Other transport services
- Post and telecommunications
- Finance
- Real estate
- Other business activities

e. Personal and Public Services

Gross Exports

Value-Added Exports

Legend:
- Public administration
- Education
- Health and social work
- Other personal services

NEC = not elsewhere classified, NRCA = normalized revealed comparative advantage.
Notes: NRCA indexes are computed according to Balassa (1965) and Yu, Cai, and Leung (2009) and multiplied by 10,000. Value-added exports are computed by summing DAVAX and REX from an origin sector decomposition of exports. DAVAX are directly absorbed value-added exports, while REX are domestic value-added exports reexported by direct importer and eventually absorbed abroad. Sector names are shortened according to Appendix 2.
Sources: Asian Development Bank (ADB). 2021. *Key Indicators for Asia and the Pacific 2021*. Manila; ADB. Multiregional Input–Output Database (accessed 14 July 2022); B. Balassa. 1965. Trade Liberalisation and "Revealed" Comparative Advantage. *The Manchester School*. 33 (2). pp. 99–123; R. Yu, J. Cai, and P. S. Leung. 2009. The Normalized Revealed Comparative Advantage Index. *Annals of Regional Science*. 43 (1). pp. 267–282; and ADB estimates.

Bangladesh's strongest comparative advantage is in the low-technology manufacturing sectors, particularly the textiles and textile products sector (Figure 4.4.b). Moreover, its comparative advantage in the sector has been growing stronger over time. Another low-technology manufacturing sector where Bangladesh has growing advantage is the leather, leather products, and footwear sector. Meanwhile, Bangladesh's more recently gained advantage in the construction sector first picked up from 2019 to 2020 but has weakened between 2020 and 2021 from both the gross exports and value-added exports approaches.

In terms of medium- to high-technology manufacturing, it is clear from Figure 4.4.c that Bangladesh has comparative disadvantage in these sectors, except from a value-added perspective in the other nonmetallic minerals sector. Except in the other nonmetallic minerals sector, Bangladesh's comparative disadvantage in these sectors has also grown stronger from 2000 to 2021. Another noticeable trend is Bangladesh's increasing comparative advantage in the wholesale trade and commission trade sector from both approaches.

Figure 4.4.d shows that Bangladesh has enjoyed a comparative advantage in the post and telecommunication sector since 2007. Moreover, the economy's advantage in this sector has grown stronger since 2007, although it has declined from its strongest comparative advantage in the sector in 2016. While Bangladesh shows a disadvantage in the financial intermediation sector under a gross exports approach, a value-added perspective shows a growing comparative advantage in the sector, highlighting its increasing importance in supporting transactions for trade.

Under personal and public services (Figure 4.4.e), Bangladesh has shown a growing comparative advantage in the public administration and defense; compulsory social security sector under both approaches. Bangladesh also appears to have growing advantage in the other community, social, and personal services sector under the value-added exports approach.

In general, increasing NRCA for several sectors across the years shows Bangladesh's increasing specialization in select sectors. Moreover, Figure 4.4 also shows that trends between gross exports and value-added exports may move in opposite directions, as in the case of the other nonmetallic minerals sector. The degree of Bangladesh's comparative advantage or disadvantage in the different sectors also varies by sector. In some sectors, comparative advantage or disadvantage is stronger under a gross exports approach, while the opposite is true in others. The difference lies in sectors' contributions to gross exports and total DAVAX and REX. Thus, it is important to understand the underlying domestic linkages that help support Bangladesh's direct exporting activities.

It is also important to understand how Bangladesh fares relative to other economies in the sectors where it has comparative advantage. Figure 4.5 draws modified box plots to compare Bangladesh's NRCA in the six sectors earlier identified as RCA sectors. In the box plots in Figure 4.5, bars represent interquartile regions, with the upper quartile being the 75th percentile and the lower quartile being the 25th percentile. Meanwhile, the upper fences represent the 90th percentile, while the lower fences represent the 10th percentile. Economies with NRCA going beyond the 90th percentile or below the 10th percentile are plotted in green dots. Bangladesh's NRCA is in orange diamonds.

Bangladesh's NRCA in the textiles and textile products sector has been above the 90th percentile since 2007. In 2000, eight economies had stronger NRCA than Bangladesh in the textiles and textile products sector using the gross exports approach, and nine economies had stronger NRCA in the sector using the value-added exports approach. These economies include Asian economies such as the People's Republic of China (PRC); the Republic of Korea; India; Taipei,China; and Indonesia. The PRC had an NRCA index using gross exports that was 6.8 times stronger and NRCA index using value-added exports that was 7.8 times stronger than Bangladesh in 2000. By 2021, the PRC's NRCA index using gross exports in the sector was 7.8 times Bangladesh's, even though Bangladesh overtook several economies and had the second strongest comparative advantage in the sector. Bangladesh's closest competitor in 2021 is Viet Nam, whose NRCA index using gross exports in the textiles and textile products sector is only 0.8 times Bangladesh's. In terms of NRCA index using value-added exports in the sector in 2021, Bangladesh ranked third, placing behind the PRC and Türkiye but still overtaking Viet Nam. Its NRCA index was less than 0.2 times that of the PRC and a little more than 0.8 times that of Türkiye's. Bangladesh's NRCA index using value-added exports in the sector is more than 1.2 times that of Viet Nam's in 2021.

Bangladesh's ranking in the post and telecommunications sector has also improved since the 2000s, with NRCA indexes increasing since 2011 under both the gross exports and value-added exports approaches. In 2000, Bangladesh ranked 39th using the gross exports approach and 34th using the value-added exports approach. In fact, in 2000, Bangladesh had a comparative disadvantage in the sector. By 2007, Bangladesh had gained comparative advantage in the sector, and by 2021, its ranking went up to 10th using the gross exports approach and 11th under the value-added exports approach. Bangladesh's NRCA index in the post and telecommunications sector was a little more than 0.2 times that of the United States under a gross exports approach and was less than 0.2 times that of the United Kingdom under a value-added exports approach.

Bangladesh has also improved its ranking in the leather, leather products, and footwear sector, where it ranked 15th in 2000 in NRCA using the gross exports approach and 17th under the value-added exports approach. By 2021, these rankings have gone up to sixth (gross exports approach) and seventh (value-added exports approach). However, the PRC's NRCA index is still about 38.9 times that of Bangladesh when using gross exports and 25.5 times when using value-added exports.

Bangladesh had a comparative disadvantage in the public administration and defense; compulsory social security sector in 2000, when its NRCA ranked 28th using gross exports and 23rd using value-added exports. By 2021, Bangladesh had ranked 10th using both approaches, as the economy built its comparative advantage in the sector over the years.

NRCA using gross exports showed that Bangladesh ranked 37th in the construction sector in 2000 when it had comparative disadvantage in the sector. On the contrary, the economy had a comparative advantage in the sector in 2000 using a value-added approach and ranked 24th. In 2021, Bangladesh showed comparative advantage in the sector under both approaches, with its ranking improving to 17th under a gross exports approach and 20th under a value-added exports approach.

Finally, among the sectors where Bangladesh has comparative advantage, the manufacturing, not elsewhere classified (NEC); recycling sector shows the weakest RCA. In 2000, when it had a comparative disadvantage in the sector, Bangladesh ranked 38th under a gross exports approach and 37th under a value-added exports approach. Its ranking improved to 19th (gross exports approach) and 16th (value-added exports approach), although it boasts of modest NRCA indexes compared with the PRC.

Overall, while Bangladesh remains a highly specialized economy, it has built comparative advantage in several sectors in recent years. However, its NRCA indexes in some sectors are still modest compared with other economies. Relatively strong comparative advantage sectors are the textiles and textile products sector; the post and telecommunications sector; and the leather, leather products, and footwear sector. The other sectors that have gained comparative advantage in recent years can still be built upon to boost diversification.

Figure 4.5: Normalized Revealed Comparative Advantage for Select Sectors, 62 Economies and Rest of the World

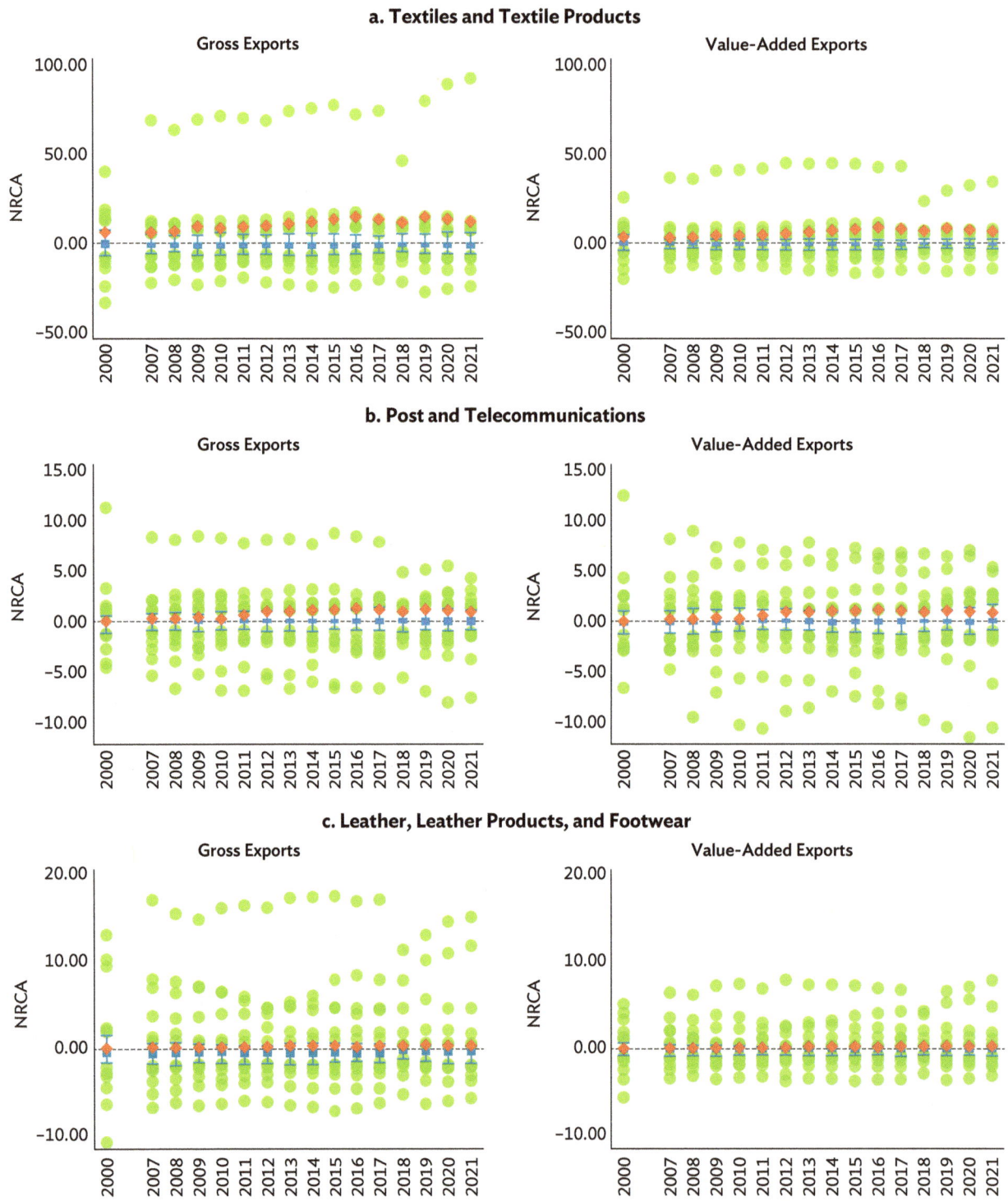

a. Textiles and Textile Products

b. Post and Telecommunications

c. Leather, Leather Products, and Footwear

continued on next page.

Figure 4.5 *continued.*

d. Public Administration and Defense; Compulsory Social Security

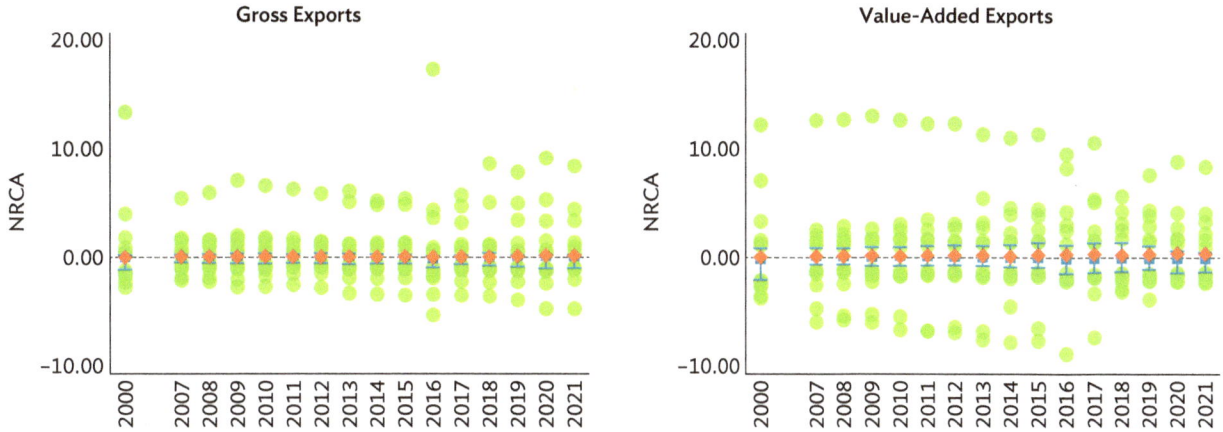

Gross Exports

Value-Added Exports

e. Construction

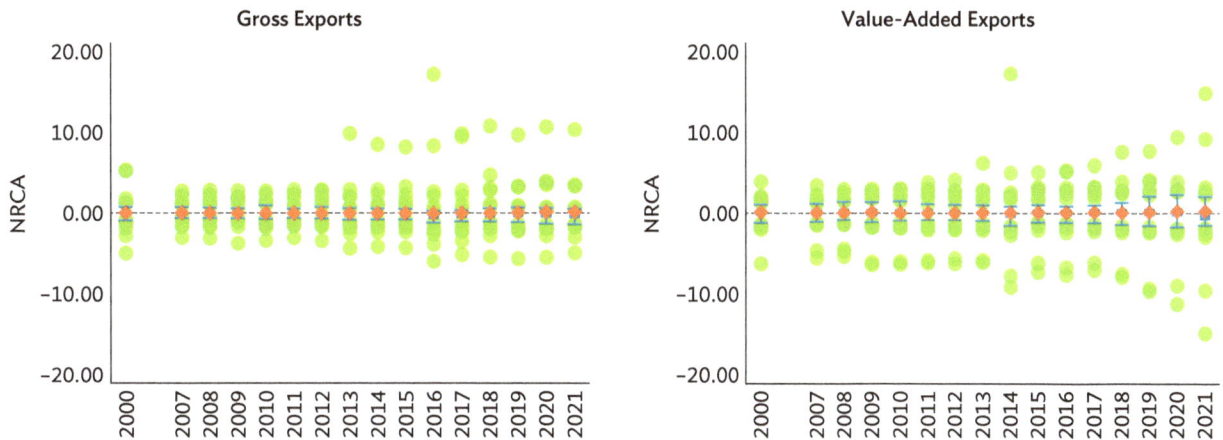

Gross Exports

Value-Added Exports

f. Manufacturing, NEC; Recycling

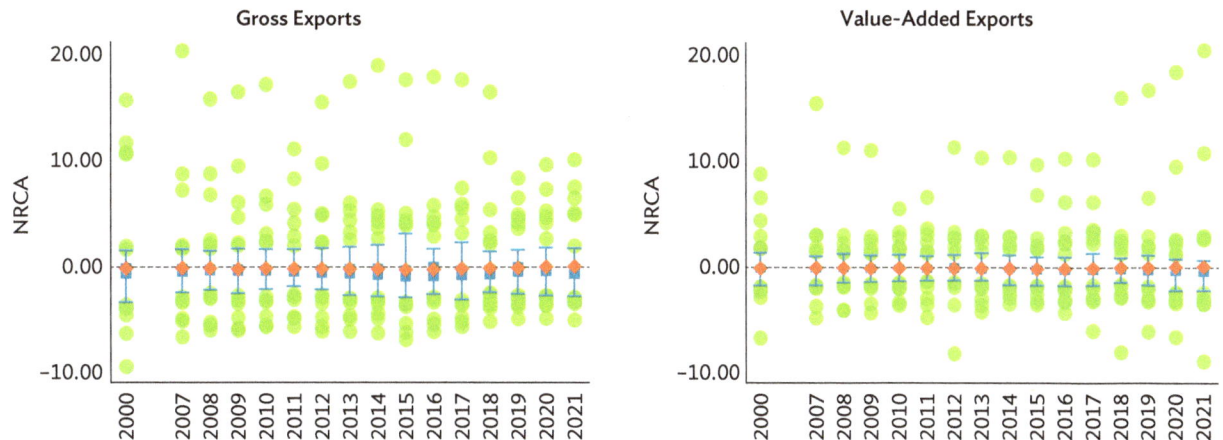

Gross Exports

Value-Added Exports

◆ Bangladesh ● Economies with NRCA above the 90th percentile and below the 10th percentile

NEC = not elsewhere classified, NRCA = normalized revealed comparative advantage.
Notes: NRCA indexes are computed according to Balassa (1965) and Yu, Cai, and Leung (2009) and multiplied by 10,000. Value-added exports are computed by summing DAVAX and REX from an origin sector decomposition of exports. DAVAX are directly absorbed value-added exports, while REX are domestic value-added exports reexported by direct importer and eventually absorbed abroad. Bars represent interquartile regions, with the upper quartile representing the 75th percentile and the lower quartile representing the 25th percentile. Upper fences represent the 90th percentile, while lower fences represent the 10th percentile.
Sources: Asian Development Bank (ADB). 2021. *Key Indicators for Asia and the Pacific 2021.* Manila; ADB. Multiregional Input–Output Database (accessed 14 July 2022); B. Balassa. 1965. Trade Liberalisation and "Revealed" Comparative Advantage. *The Manchester School.* 33 (2). pp. 99–123; R. Yu, J. Cai, and P. S. Leung. 2009. The Normalized Revealed Comparative Advantage Index. *Annals of Regional Science.* 43 (1). pp. 267–282; and ADB estimates.

C.   Agglomeration

While GVC participation is important in determining how integrated an economy-sector is within a value chain, it does not guarantee gains from participation (Kummritz 2016; Taglioni and Winkler 2016). Discussions on gains from GVCs often focus on upgrading priority sectors toward higher value-added segments of the chain. Meanwhile, the role of domestic sectors is given less focus. However, strong linkages between domestic sectors and those participating in GVCs imply that domestic sectors contribute to GVCs by providing intermediate inputs or absorbing value-added through consumption. In fact, traditional indicators of GVCs are unable to capture the complex relationship between domestic linkages and GVCs (Mercer-Blackman, Foronda, and Mariasingham 2017; Bernard et al. 2007).

In the case of Bangladesh, measuring domestic linkages complements previous analyses by taking into account the role of domestic sectors in GVCs. This has especially risen in importance in recent years, as firms, once outsourcing parts of their production process, have started to "reshore" or "near-shore" to cushion against risks in global supply chains (ADB 2022b). Vulnerabilities arising from different types of shocks, such as the COVID-19 pandemic and geopolitical conflicts, raise the importance of measuring domestic linkages to make GVCs more resilient.

Interpreting domestic linkages as the tendency of economic activities to "locate" domestically, this section adapts a value-added-based measure of agglomeration. This captures how much value-added is sourced from and/or absorbed by domestic sectors relative to the rest of the world. As such, the value-added-based measure of agglomeration differs from traditional measures of agglomeration, which can be hard to obtain as they utilize either firm location or employment data (Baris et al. 2022). The index is derived from the value-added decomposition framework of Wang et al. (2017b). The analysis starts with the construction of a VBY matrix, which depicts the distribution of value-added across economy-sectors. Column elements of this matrix correspond to the total final goods (Y) produced by an economy-sector. The backward agglomeration index captures the contribution of domestic sectors to the total final goods and compares it to the global average for the sector. Thus, an economy-sector with high backward agglomeration ($AGG_B > 1$) implies that, on average, its final good is comprised largely of domestic value-added (DVA). Meanwhile, row elements of the VBY matrix correspond to the gross value-added (GVA) of an economy-sector. From this, the forward agglomeration index captures the share of an economy's GVA that is absorbed by domestic sectors. Simply put, high forward agglomeration ($AGG_F > 1$) implies that the value-added generated is driven by domestic consumption.

Both backward and forward agglomeration indexes can be used to form four agglomeration classes that describe an economy-sector's state of agglomeration. For low agglomeration economies ($AGG_B < 1, AGG_F < 1$), the contribution of DVA to final goods production is smaller than the global average, and domestic consumption is not the primary driver of value-added generated. Meanwhile, DVA-generating economy-sectors ($AGG_B < 1, AGG_F > 1$) are domestically agglomerated in the forward sense—they produce valuable goods for the domestic market consumption. On the other hand, export-oriented, domestic sourcing economies ($AGG_B > 1, AGG_F < 1$) source their inputs domestically to produce goods for the external market. When an economy-sector has both high backward and forward agglomeration ($AGG_B > 1, AGG_F > 1$), the economy-sector is said to be highly agglomerated (Figure 4.6).

Figure 4.6: The Agglomeration Map

EDS Economies $AGG_B > 1$, $AGG_F < 1$	High Agglomeration $AGG_B > 1$, $AGG_F > 1$
Low Agglomeration $AGG_B < 1$, $AGG_F < 1$	DVA-Generating Economies $AGG_B < 1$, $AGG_F > 1$

AGG_B = backward agglomeration index; AGG_F = forward agglomeration index; DVA = domestic value-added; EDS = export-oriented, domestic sourcing.
Source: Authors' illustration.

The agglomeration indexes can be used to look at the strength of domestic linkages for Bangladesh relative to other economies. Bangladesh is in the upper right quadrant of the agglomeration map in Figure 4.7, implying that it has been a high-agglomeration economy over the years. In the backward sense, this implies that the contribution of the domestic sectors to the final goods produced in Bangladesh is higher than the global average. At the same time, GVA in Bangladesh is primarily consumed and/or absorbed by domestic sectors, making Bangladesh agglomerated in the forward sense. While there is no change in agglomeration class over time, the magnitude of indexes has changed over the years. Between 2007 and 2014, Bangladesh exhibited a decline in overall agglomeration, which recovered and improved between 2014 and 2021.

The role of domestic linkages takes on a different depth when Bangladesh is compared with other economies. Bangladesh exhibits higher agglomeration than Viet Nam, which has been a low-agglomeration economy for the selected periods. Meanwhile, Pakistan shows higher values for the agglomeration indexes than Bangladesh, implying that domestic sectors in Pakistan play a larger role in production and consumption relative to Bangladesh. This reflects internal policies in Pakistan that aim to increase DVA (Dollar et al. 2020).

The agglomeration indexes also allow for a sector-specific analysis. Focusing on the textiles and textile products sector, which dominates total exports in Bangladesh, it is easy to see that Bangladesh's textiles sector exhibits low agglomeration (Figure 4.8). In the backward sense, this means that relative to other economies, the textiles and textile products sector in Bangladesh does not rely on intermediate inputs sourced domestically. Concurrently, low forward agglomeration suggests that the domestic consumption of textiles is not a major driver in the generation of value-added for this sector.

The textiles and textile product sectors in Viet Nam and Cambodia belong to the same agglomeration class, in contrast to India and Pakistan. India's textiles sector exhibits high agglomeration in both periods, while Pakistan's moves from a high agglomeration class in 2007 toward an export-oriented, domestic sourcing class in 2021. In both economies, domestic sectors play a larger role in the textiles sector, either as the main contributor to final goods (backward agglomeration) or as the main driver of value-added generation (forward agglomeration). Looking at the levels of the indexes, however, both backward and forward agglomeration are declining for Viet Nam and Pakistan but increasing for Bangladesh. This suggests that domestic sectors may play a larger role in the textiles sector of Bangladesh in the future.

Figure 4.7: Economy–Level Agglomeration Map, 2007, 2014, and 2021

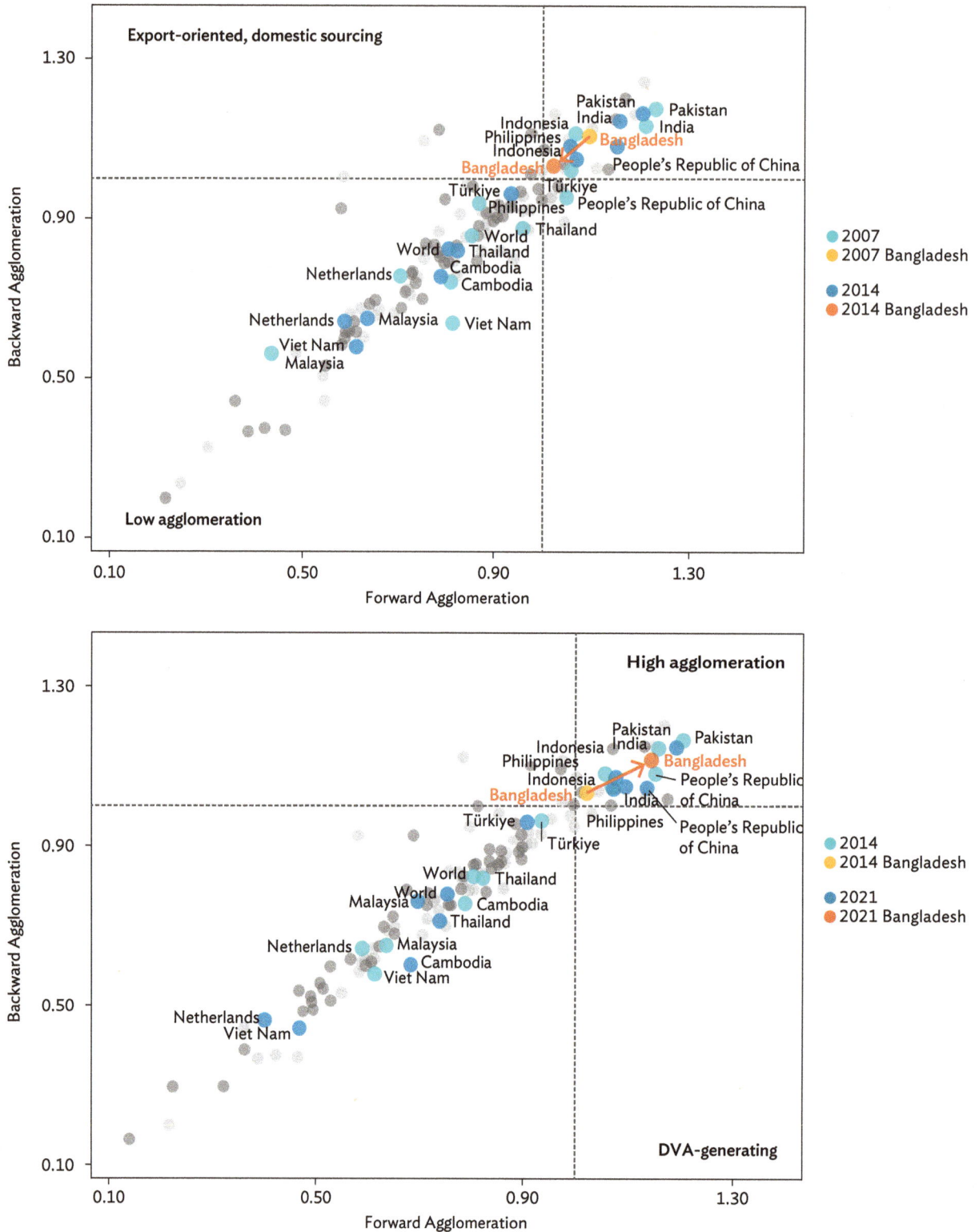

Top panel (x-axis: Forward Agglomeration, y-axis: Backward Agglomeration)

Export-oriented, domestic sourcing

Pakistan, India, Pakistan, Indonesia, Philippines, Indonesia, Bangladesh, Bangladesh, People's Republic of China, Türkiye, Philippines, People's Republic of China, Thailand, World, Thailand, Cambodia, Cambodia, Netherlands, Netherlands, Malaysia, Viet Nam, Viet Nam, Malaysia

Low agglomeration

Legend:
- 2007
- 2007 Bangladesh
- 2014
- 2014 Bangladesh

Bottom panel (x-axis: Forward Agglomeration, y-axis: Backward Agglomeration)

High agglomeration

Pakistan, India, Pakistan, Indonesia, Philippines, Indonesia, Bangladesh, Bangladesh, People's Republic of China, India, Philippines, People's Republic of China, Türkiye, Türkiye, World, World, Thailand, Malaysia, Cambodia, Thailand, Netherlands, Malaysia, Cambodia, Viet Nam, Netherlands, Viet Nam

DVA-generating

Legend:
- 2014
- 2014 Bangladesh
- 2021
- 2021 Bangladesh

DVA = domestic value-added.
Note: The values are computed based on the framework presented in Baris et al. (2022) and aggregated at an economy level.
Sources: Asian Development Bank (ADB). Multiregional Input–Output Database (accessed 26 October 2022); K. V. Baris, M. C. R. Crisostomo, K. A. V. Garay, C. R. J. Jabagat, M. J. Mariasingham, and E. M. T. Mores. 2022. Measuring Localization in the Age of Economic Globalization. *ADB Economics Working Paper Series*. No. 647. Manila: ADB; and ADB estimates.

Figure 4.8: Agglomeration Map for the Textiles and Textile Products Sector, 2007 and 2021

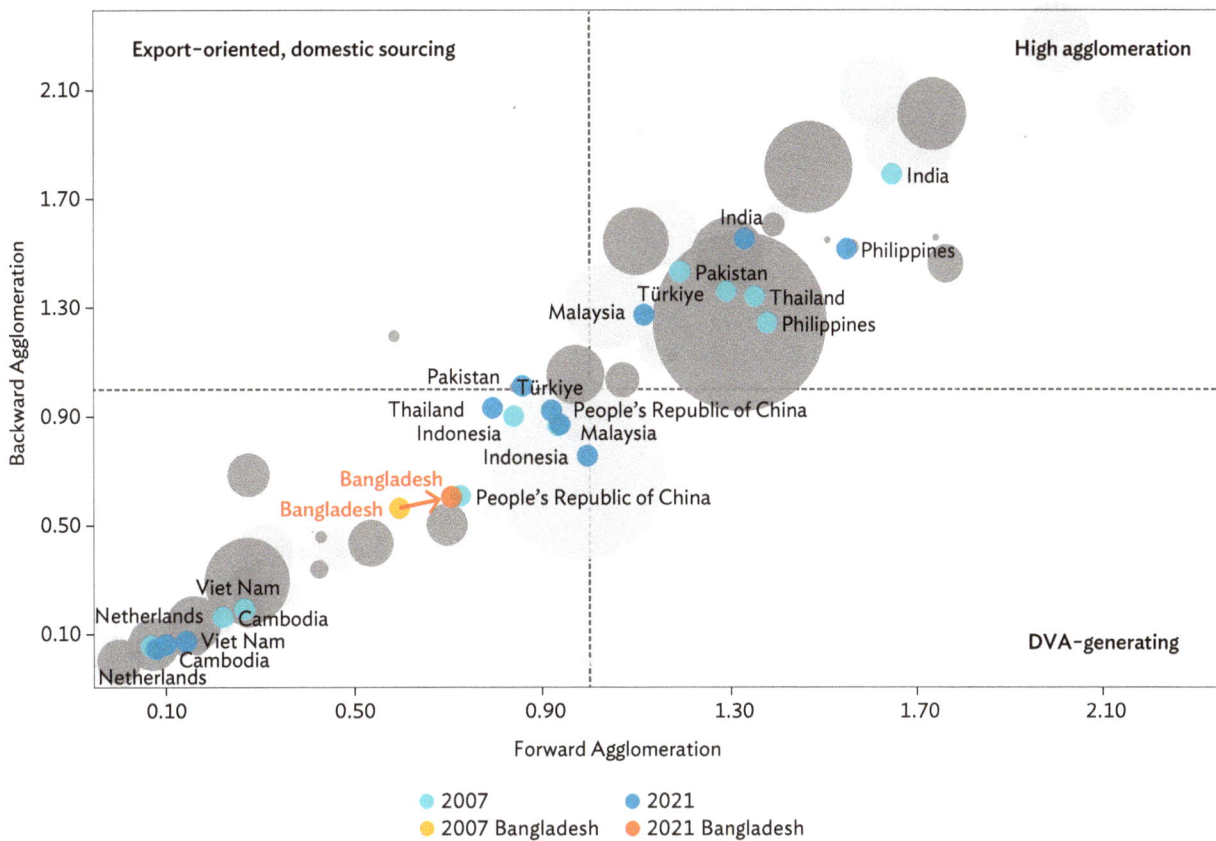

Notes: The values are computed based on the framework presented in Baris et al. (2022). Bubble size indicates gross value-added.
Sources: Asian Development Bank (ADB). Multiregional Input–Output Database (accessed 26 October 2022); K. V. Baris, M. C. R. Crisostomo, K. A. V. Garay, C. R. J. Jabagat, M. J. Mariasingham, and E. M. T. Mores. 2022. Measuring Localization in the Age of Economic Globalization. *ADB Economics Working Paper Series.* No. 647. Manila: ADB; and ADB estimates.

The agglomeration indexes can be utilized to compare domestic linkages across sectors in Bangladesh. Using the 35-sector disaggregation, Figure 4.9 maps the agglomeration indexes for all sectors in Bangladesh for selected years. Sectors with a backward agglomeration index greater than one has high backward agglomeration. The interpretation for forward agglomeration is analogous. Consistent with the previous discussion, the textiles and textile products sector shows low forward and backward agglomeration. However, both indexes depict an increasing trend.

Data for the other sectors show that the electrical and optical equipment sector stands out as one of the sectors with the largest increase in backward agglomeration. In 2007, its backward agglomeration index was at 1.13, increasing to 1.35 in 2014 and reaching 3.06 in 2021. This suggests an increasing role for DVA in the production of final goods in Bangladesh's electrical sectors. Meanwhile, sectors such as paper, refined fuels, rubber and plastics, air transport, and water transport exhibit declines in backward agglomeration. Among these sectors, water transport has recorded the largest decline in backward agglomeration, followed by refined fuels.

Figure 4.9: Bangladesh Sector-Level Agglomeration, 2007, 2014, and 2021

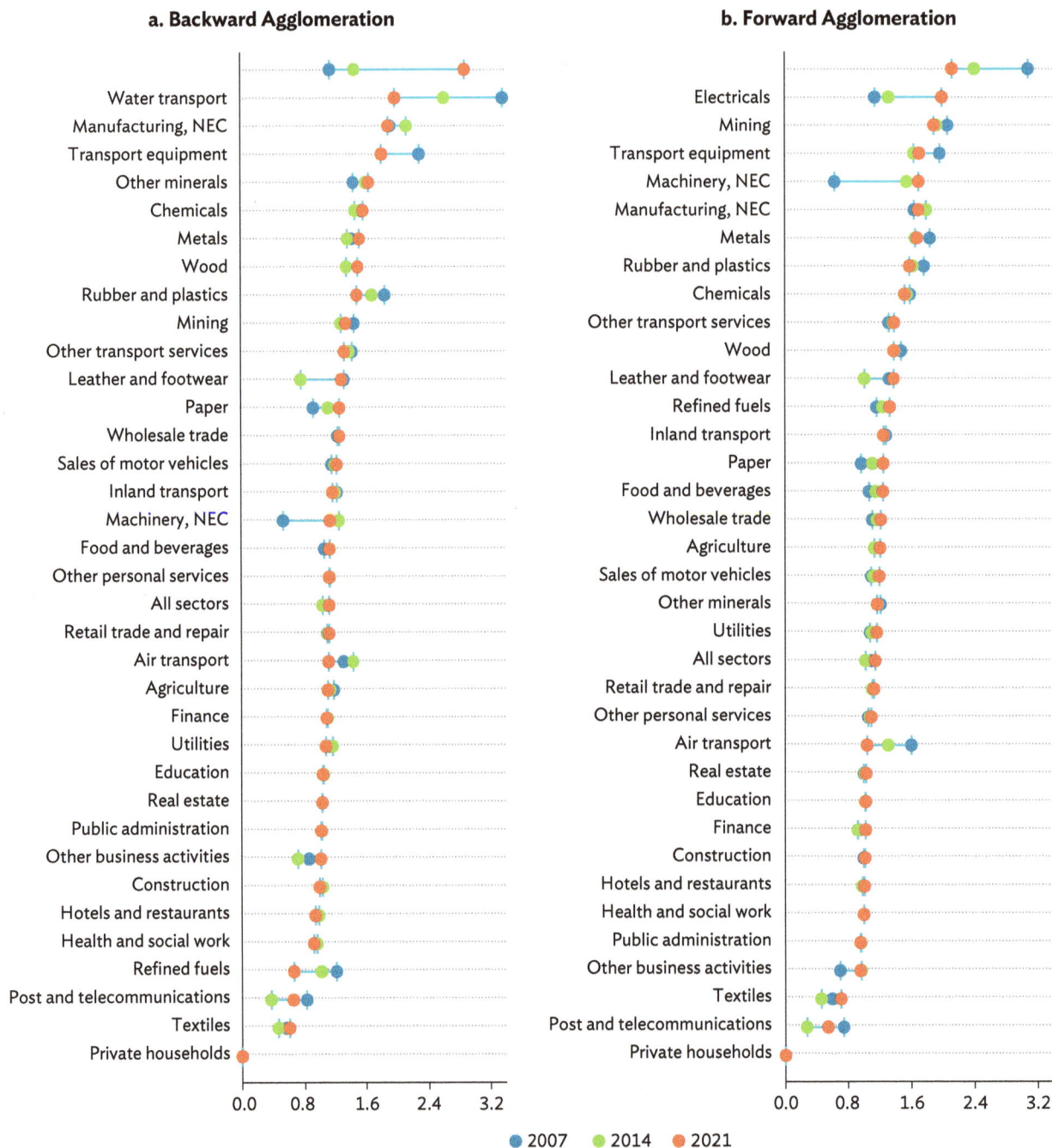

a. Backward Agglomeration

Water transport
Manufacturing, NEC
Transport equipment
Other minerals
Chemicals
Metals
Wood
Rubber and plastics
Mining
Other transport services
Leather and footwear
Paper
Wholesale trade
Sales of motor vehicles
Inland transport
Machinery, NEC
Food and beverages
Other personal services
All sectors
Retail trade and repair
Air transport
Agriculture
Finance
Utilities
Education
Real estate
Public administration
Other business activities
Construction
Hotels and restaurants
Health and social work
Refined fuels
Post and telecommunications
Textiles
Private households

0.0   0.8   1.6   2.4   3.2

b. Forward Agglomeration

Electricals
Mining
Transport equipment
Machinery, NEC
Manufacturing, NEC
Metals
Rubber and plastics
Chemicals
Other transport services
Wood
Leather and footwear
Refined fuels
Inland transport
Paper
Food and beverages
Wholesale trade
Agriculture
Sales of motor vehicles
Other minerals
Utilities
All sectors
Retail trade and repair
Other personal services
Air transport
Real estate
Education
Finance
Construction
Hotels and restaurants
Health and social work
Public administration
Other business activities
Textiles
Post and telecommunications
Private households

0.0   0.8   1.6   2.4   3.2

● 2007   ● 2014   ● 2021

NEC = not elsewhere classified.
Notes: The values are computed based on the framework presented in Baris et al. (2022). Sector names are shortened according to Appendix 2.
Sources: Asian Development Bank (ADB). Multiregional Input–Output Database (accessed 26 October 2022); K. V. Baris, M. C. R. Crisostomo, K. A. V. Garay, C. R. J. Jabagat, M. J. Mariasingham, and E. M. T. Mores. 2022. Measuring Localization in the Age of Economic Globalization. *ADB Economics Working Paper Series*. No. 647. Manila: ADB; and ADB estimates.

Similarly, the electrical and optical equipment sector records the highest increase in forward agglomeration over time, growing from 1.08 in 2007 to 2.06 in 2021. This implies that domestic sectors have increasingly absorbed value-added generated by the electrical and optical equipment sector in Bangladesh. The machinery, NEC sector exhibits a similar trend, allowing the sector to shift from low forward agglomeration in 2007 (with a value of 0.63) to high forward agglomeration (with a value of 1.74). In contrast, the forward agglomeration indexes of the transport sectors, such as air and water transport, and the rubber and plastics sector have declined over time.

Agglomeration indexes provide another layer of analysis when focus is given to sectors where Bangladesh has a comparative advantage. As previously discussed, these sectors include (i) textiles and textile products; (ii) post and telecommunications; (iii) leather, leather products, and footwear; (iv) public administration and defense; compulsory social work; (v) construction; and (vi) manufacturing, NEC. Both the textiles and textile products sector and the post and telecommunications sector are low-agglomeration sectors. Meanwhile, the manufacturing, NEC sector has consistently belonged to the high-agglomeration class, implying that this sector has strong domestic linkages in the backward and forward sense. The public administration and defense; compulsory social work sector exhibits high backward agglomeration, implying that a significant portion of its final goods comes from domestic value-added.

Construction, in the meantime, exhibits changes in agglomeration classes over the years. In 2007, it had low forward agglomeration (AGG_F = 0.99), which increased to high forward agglomeration in 2014 (AGG_F = 1.012) and remained at almost the same level in 2021. On the other hand, it shifted from high backward agglomeration in 2014 (AGG_B = 1.03) to low backward agglomeration (AGG_B = 0.99) in 2021. This implies that, between 2007 and 2021, its agglomeration class changed from an export-oriented domestic sourcing sector to a DVA-generating sector.

Overall, this illustrates that Bangladesh has strong domestic linkages relative to other economies. However, the strength of domestic linkages varies across sectors. Textiles, its main export, continues to have low agglomeration, suggesting a limited role for the domestic sectors in terms of production. However, high agglomeration in the other sectors, such as electrical and optical equipment, influences the level of agglomeration in Bangladesh. Whether this trend impacts the resilience of GVCs within Bangladesh amid the current and potential risks in the global supply chain presents an area for future exploration.

Chapter 5

LEAST-DEVELOPED COUNTRY GRADUATION, PREFERENCE EROSION, AND GEOGRAPHICAL DIVERSIFICATION

While productivity growth and the ascent to higher levels of income classification are typically deemed as significant landmarks in the development narrative of economies, some growing pains may be experienced along the way. In the case of Bangladesh, the impending graduation from the status of least developed country (LDC) in November 2026 poses a considerable challenge as this simultaneously marks the discontinuation of benefits granted by preferential trading schemes, most notably the European Union's Everything but Arms (EBA) agreement.

Like many of its Asian counterparts, the economy took extensive advantage of unilateral and nonreciprocal duty- and quota-free market access to bolster its trade performance and eventually become a major player in the exchange of ready-made garments (RMG), translating to around 90% of Bangladesh's exports in recent years (Kumar 2022). It is important to note, however, that more favorable rules of origin also facilitated this development—a key argument raised by LDCs in their WTO submissions and ministerial declarations since 2015 (Crivelli and Inama 2021).

In 2011, the EBA reform was implemented, which allowed single transformation (i.e., fabrics to finished knitted or crocheted garments) and, consequently, the use of non-originating fabric from the People's Republic of China (PRC) in the production of garments by Bangladesh. This made compliance simpler for the economy and led to substantial increases in preference utilization related to the European Union (EU) (ADB 2022a Box 3.3). As seen in Figure 5.1, the rate gradually increased from around 60% in 2002 to almost 80% in 2010 before jumping to above 90% immediately following the reform. Meanwhile, utilization rates having North American export destinations displayed general downtrends. United States (US) Generalized System of Trade Preferences (GSP), which does not cover RMGs, had considerably less trade values of covered imports compared to the EU, possibly explaining the more volatile trend.

The increased RMG exports to the EU accounted for about 96% utilization rate of the EBA scheme in 2021. To put this into context, this means that of the $17.3 billion worth of textile products sent to the EU, around $16.5 billion were exempted from import duties, sales, or other taxes (ADB 2022a). On the flipside, it is this considerable amount of duty savings that is being threatened by the looming preference erosion. Barring any transitory granting of preferences and rerouting of trade to alternative markets, a deceleration in the growth of Bangladesh's exports may soon transpire, thus making it valuable to explore the economy's current menu of adjustment options related to this crucial development. At the same time, Bangladesh has shown its ability to compete in the US market despite the absence of trade preferences for RMG exports, not covered by the US GSP scheme.[5] It remains to be seen whether Bangladeshi exporters will be able to maintain their market shares in the EU while paying MFN duties, facing competition from other economies benefiting from free market access, such as Viet Nam for example.

---

[5] The US GSP expired on 31 December 2020. Discussions on its renewal are ongoing as of this writing.

Figure 5.1: Bangladesh GSP Utilization Rates of Textile and Textile Articles, 2005–2020
(%)

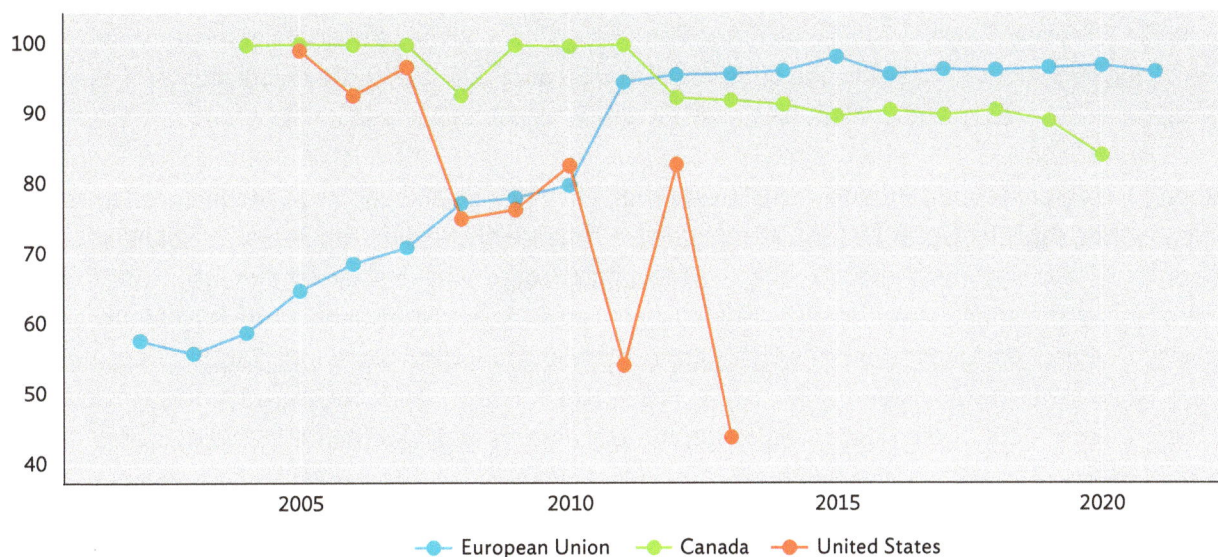

GSP = Generalized System of Trade Preferences.
Source: United Nations Conference on Trade and Development. Database on GSP Utilization (accessed 20 November 2022).

At this stage, Bangladesh can retain the geographical structure of its exports by applying for other preferences under the EU or initiate modifications and expand market access by entering new treaties such as regional trade agreements. In the 2022 Aid for Trade report of the Asian Development Bank (ADB), it is mentioned that there is an option to apply for the EU's Special Incentive Arrangement for Sustainable Development and Good Governance (GSP+). However, duty-free market access under the GSP+ is subject to a less favorable set of rules of origin compared to the EBA and will be granted only upon compliance with a series of non-trade conditionalities. Since the production structure has an established dependence on foreign-sourced fabric, looking for local suppliers offering comparable levels of quality at reasonable prices will be imperative during the period preceding the transition. Otherwise, clothing exports might fall back to default GSP status with applicable tariffs of around 8.0%–9.3% or even higher. In either case, it will be challenging to maintain the same level of exports to the EU, especially considering how consistently high preference utilization rates have been in recent times.

As mentioned above, another option is to consider joining or negotiating trade agreements that could not only provide alternative market access upon graduation (ADB 2022a) but also be an integral part of the adjustment/coping strategies for the loss of trade preferences through the reduction of trade barriers on imports of inputs, thereby compensating for increased overall costs of exporting and maintaining/increasing the competitiveness of industries. An example of a favorable agreement for Bangladesh is one that would allow the economy to import yarn or fabrics duty free, thus offsetting a portion of tariffs paid when exporting RMGs to the EU. Recently enforced open trade agreements in Asia are the Regional Comprehensive Economic Partnership (RCEP) and the Comprehensive and Progressive Agreement for Trans-Pacific Partnership (CPTPP). The RCEP is a free trade agreement (FTA) among the 10 Association of Southeast Asian Nations (ASEAN) member states and their main FTA partners, namely Australia, the PRC, Japan,

New Zealand, and the Republic of Korea with a framework based on the lowering of trade barriers such as tariffs and red tape as well as improving market access for products in the East Asia region (according to the ASEAN Secretariat). On the other hand, the CPTPP is a trade agreement among Canada, Australia, Japan, Mexico, New Zealand, Singapore, Viet Nam, and Peru, which incorporates a majority of provisions from the Trans-Pacific Partnership. These include preferential market access, enhanced measures for transparency, predictability, consistency, and unified rules of origin (Government of Canada 2022).

Entering such agreements or negotiating bilateral ones will hinge on an economy's technical competence and negotiating capacity (ADB 2022a). Thus, economic planners and decision-makers of Bangladesh must carefully plan out which opportunities are most practical to pursue given limited resources. This can be done by assessing the historical performances of trade agreements and identifying the most promising alternative destinations of its highly concentrated goods (exports-wise). For the assessment of trade agreements' historical performances, as more data becomes available, the economy can look into the preference utilization rates of regional trade agreements to gauge their effectiveness and determine which ones are more valuable for improving market access and regulatory convergence (Crivelli and Inama 2021). Low rates may indicate the existence of factors that hinder the utilization of regional trade agreements, such as less favorable rules of origin, high compliance costs, and complex technological requirements. On the other hand, high rates also warrant careful investigation as this may conceal low volumes of trade as well as narrow coverages of preferential agreements (ADB 2022a, UNCTAD 2021b). Nonetheless, preference utilization rates are still useful starting metrics for specifying a few viable options among a slew of overlapping trade agreements.

In terms of widening the geographical diversification of export destinations, Crivelli (2022) proposed a simple methodology that can be used by LDCs or any other economy facing issues of highly concentrated exports as a template. It only involves three main steps: (i) identifying products of concern, (ii) identifying top export destinations for products of concern, and (iii) identifying alternative markets. For the first step, export data of Bangladesh at the Harmonized System (HS) 2 level is used to derive Herfindahl–Hirschman indexes (HHIs) and identify highly concentrated goods. As seen in Figure 5.2, many of Bangladesh's commodity exports were highly concentrated throughout the years, but all of these only comprised a small portion (<1%) of the economy's total exports. Two categories were clear outliers, namely HS 61 (apparel and clothing accessories; knitted or crocheted) and HS 62 (apparel and clothing accessories; not knitted or crocheted), with export shares close to or above 40%. Although the HHIs of both appear to be relatively low (0.08 for HS 61 and 0.14 for HS 62), a more careful examination of their destinations (step 2) suggest a considerable level of concentration.

Figure 5.3 (page 52 to 53) shows the top destinations of Bangladesh's HS 61 and HS 62 exports. With the exception of the United States (US), Canada, and Australia, all the main partners for HS 61 were from the EU.[6] This is consistent with the narrative of extensive utilization of the EBA, especially after the reform that allowed single transformation. Exports to Germany, for example, increased almost threefold from 2005 ($800.0 million) to 2015 ($2.5 billion), a few years after the enforcement of more favorable rules of origin. With regard to HS 62 exports, reliance on preferences is also evident. EU economies such as Germany, the United Kingdom (UK), France, Italy, and Spain also received considerable amounts of HS 62 products from Bangladesh.

---

[6]   The United Kingdom left the EU on 31 January 2020.

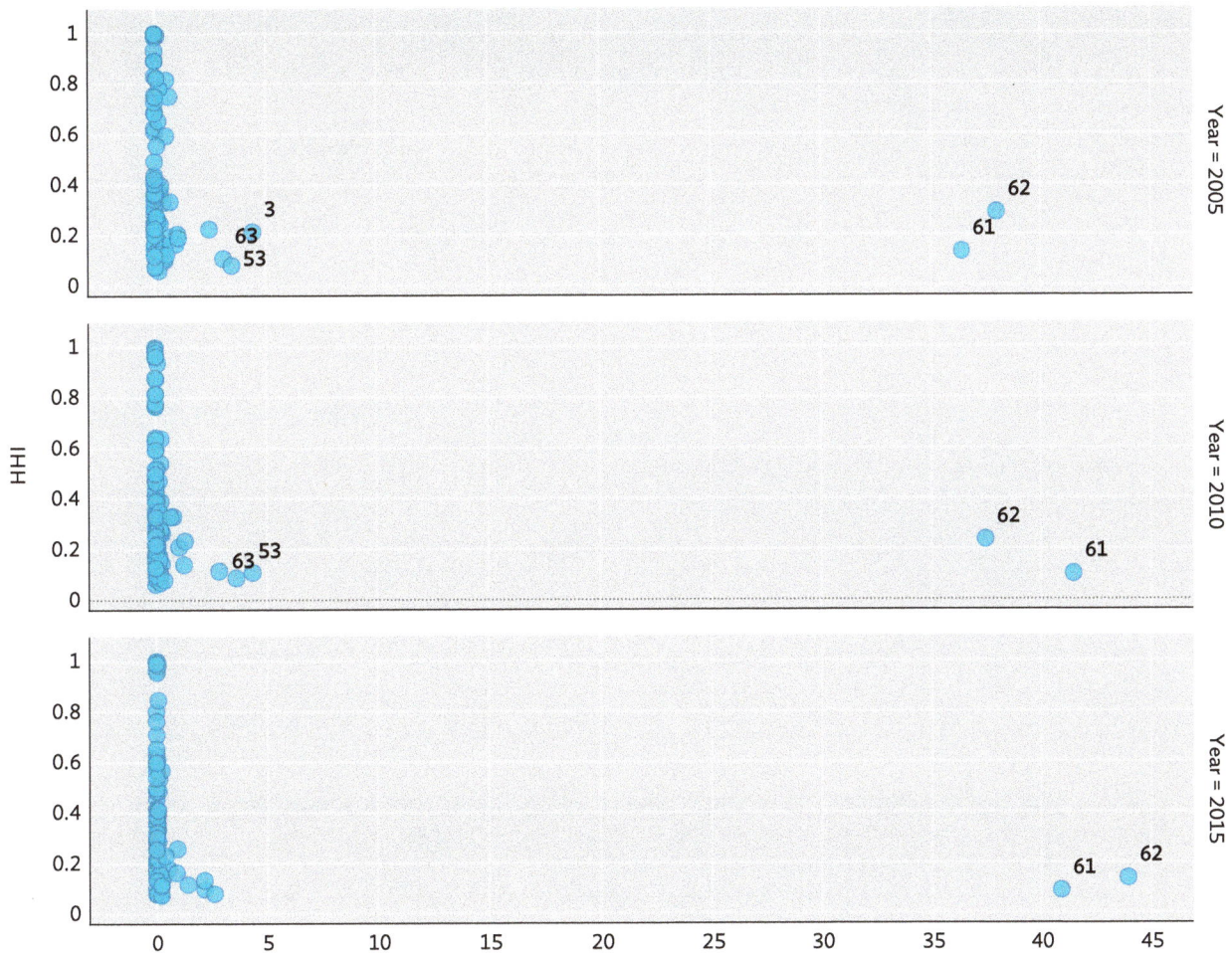

Figure 5.2: Bangladesh HHI and Export Shares by Commodity (Harmonized System 2), 2005, 2010, and 2015
(% of exports)

HHI = Herfindahl–Hirschman Index.
Note: HHIs and export shares are computed for 2-digit product lines using the Harmonized System revision year as reported.
Sources: United Nations. Comtrade Database (accessed 20 November 2022); and Asian Development Bank estimates.

North American destinations were also seen in the top ranks. Even in the absence of trade preferences for RMG, the US remained as the first export market destination for Bangladesh's HS 62 exports. Canada, on the other hand, ranked 10th in 2000 before climbing several spots in the following years, which came after the addition of apparel to its General Preferential Tariff (GPT) regulation as well as the reform in the rules of origin in 2003 (UNCTAD 2021b, UNCTAD 2021c). Interestingly, Japan, which also provides trade preferences to Bangladesh and is a member of both the RCEP and CPTPP, is seen to be one of the main partners for trade of these commodities. Following the post-graduation loss of trade preferences that Bangladesh will incur when exporting to Japan, negotiating entry in one of the mega-regionals or a bilateral agreement can be considered as a potential avenue for maintaining or expanding market shares.

Figure 5.3: Bangladesh Top Harmonized Systems 61 and 62 Export Destinations, 2000–2015

HS 61

2000 ($ million)

United States	
Germany	
France	
United Kingdom	
Netherlands	
Belgium	
Italy	
Sweden	
Denmark	
Canada	

(axis: 0, 50, 100, 150, 200, 250, 300)

2005 ($ million)

Germany	
United States	
France	
United Kingdom	
Spain	
Italy	
Canada	
Netherlands	
Belgium	
Sweden	

(axis: 0, 100, 200, 300, 400, 500, 600, 700, 800)

2010 ($ billion)

Germany	
United States	
United Kingdom	
France	
Netherlands	
Spain	
Italy	
Canada	
Türkiye	
Denmark	

(axis: 0, 0.2, 0.4, 0.6, 0.8, 1.0, 1.2, 1.4, 1.6)

2015 ($ billion)

Germany	
United Kingdom	
United States	
France	
Spain	
Italy	
Belgium	
Canada	
Denmark	
Australia	

(axis: 0, 0.5, 1.0, 1.5, 2.0, 2.5)

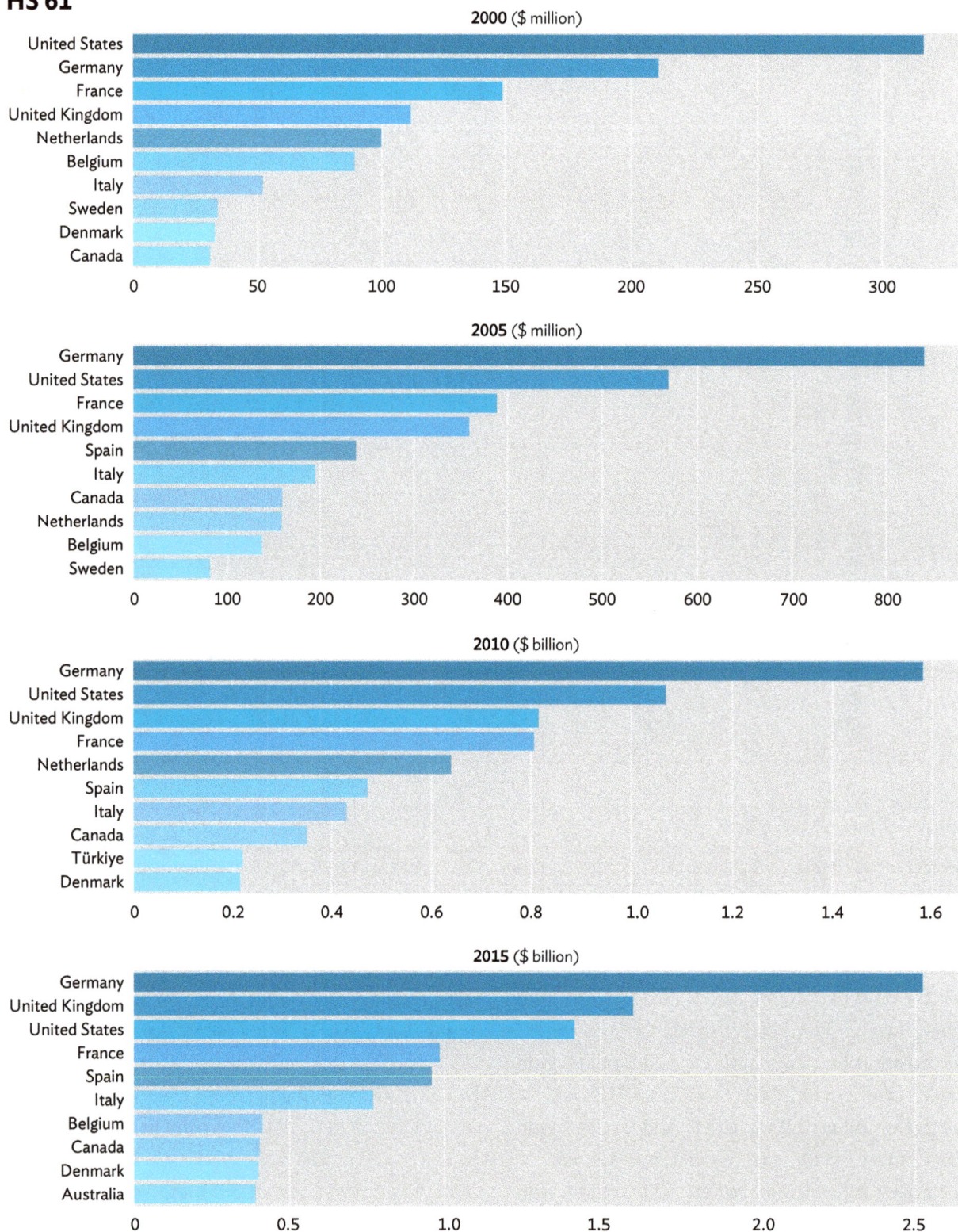

continued on next page.

Figure 5.3 *continued.*

HS 62

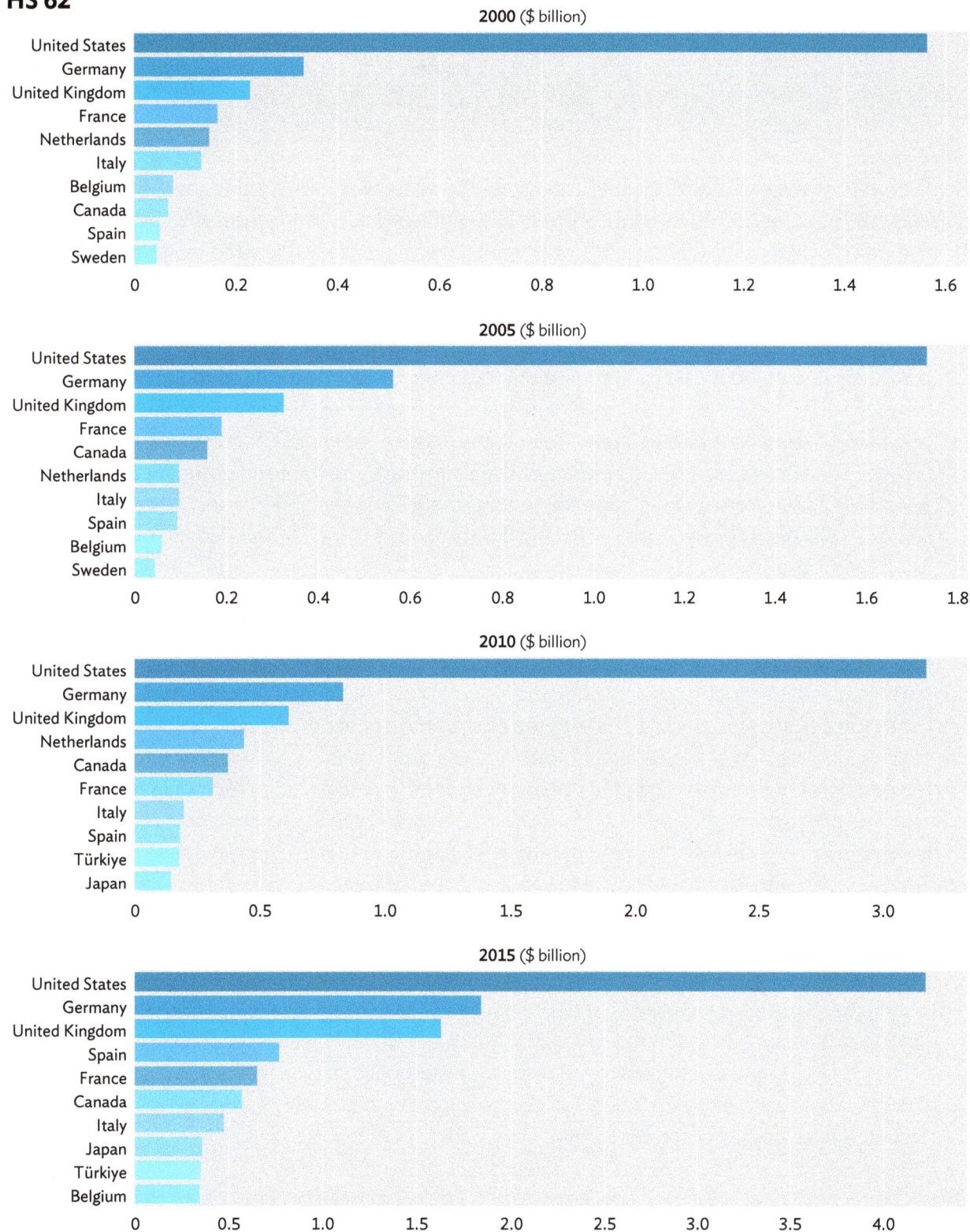

2000 ($ billion)

United States, Germany, United Kingdom, France, Netherlands, Italy, Belgium, Canada, Spain, Sweden

2005 ($ billion)

United States, Germany, United Kingdom, France, Canada, Netherlands, Italy, Spain, Belgium, Sweden

2010 ($ billion)

United States, Germany, United Kingdom, Netherlands, Canada, France, Italy, Spain, Türkiye, Japan

2015 ($ billion)

United States, Germany, United Kingdom, Spain, France, Canada, Italy, Japan, Türkiye, Belgium

HS = harmonized system.
Note: HS 61 refers to "articles of apparel and clothing accessories, knitted or crocheted," while HS 62 refers to "articles of apparel and clothing accessories, not knitted or crocheted."
Sources: United Nations. Comtrade Database (accessed 20 November 2022); and Asian Development Bank estimates.

Having established that Bangladesh has a level of concentration in HS 61 and HS 62 commodities in terms of export shares and destinations, the next step is to identify new, alternative destinations for these products based on relative import shares (RIS) defined by the equation below:

$$RIS_{i,r} = \left(\frac{imports_{i,r}}{\sum_i imports_{i,r}}\right) \Bigg/ \left(\frac{\sum_r imports_{i,r}}{\sum_i \sum_r imports_{i,r}}\right)$$

where i corresponds to commodity classification and r to economy. Intuitively, this gives the extent of import dependence of an economy for a particular commodity by comparing the national share of the said commodity in total exports versus the global figure. Any value above one signifies dependence, with higher values corresponding to increased reliance on foreign sources.

In Figure 5.4, the top export destinations with relative HS 61 and 62 import shares above one are shown. The top partners of Bangladesh for both commodity categories, which correspond to the orange-colored bars, also appeared to be the top export destinations among import dependent economies in 2021. For HS 61, alternative markets include Japan, Poland, the Russian Federation, Switzerland, and Austria. On the other hand, current top trading partners of Bangladesh are also the main destinations for HS 62 exports in 2021. Alternatives include members of the RCEP and CPTPP, namely the Republic of Korea and Australia, respectively, as well as Poland, Switzerland, and the Russian Federation.

There could be an opportunity for Bangladesh to intensify its trade of HS 61 and HS 62 products to Japan given its pre-existing trading relationships with the economy. However, graduation will also lead to a loss in trade preferences.[7] This, coupled with the size of the Japanese market for RMGs, reinforces the opportuneness of negotiating an agreement that could facilitate trade redirection from the EU in case of unsuccessful attemps to sign FTAs with the bloc. It may appear that Poland and Austria are not as viable since they are part of the EU, and exports to these economies are therefore affected by the coming graduation. On the other hand, the LDC graduation of Bangladesh may likely lead to preference erosion with respect to other (i.e., non-EU) European economies such as Switzerland. It remains to be seen, however, up to what extent the economy can remain relevant in the European market as it did in North America even with the impending trade barriers, given the uneven playing field with respect to some of its competitors.

As for the Russian Federation, the uncertainties surrounding the Russian invasion of Ukraine together with the numerous sanctions imposed on the economy may make respective plans for trade diversion not appealing at the moment. Lastly, the position of RCEP and CPTPP member economies in the upper echelon of HS 61 and 62 recipients worldwide may present additional justification for pursuing negotiations related to these treaties subject of course to proper evaluation of existing realities and legislations as well as viability of market access.

---

[7] GSP utilization rate of HS 61 and 62 products were at 94.98% and 95.60%, respectively in 2021.

Figure 5.4: Key Harmonized Systems 61 and 62 Export Destinations, 2021
($ billion)

HS 61

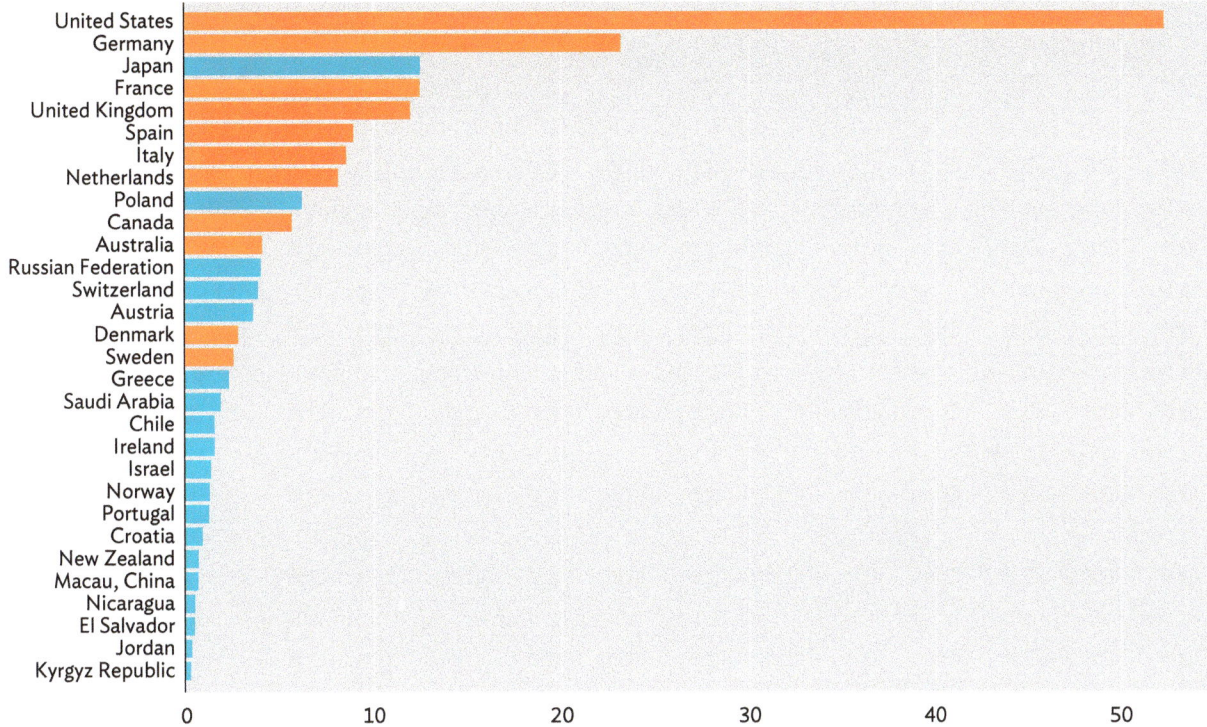

HS 62

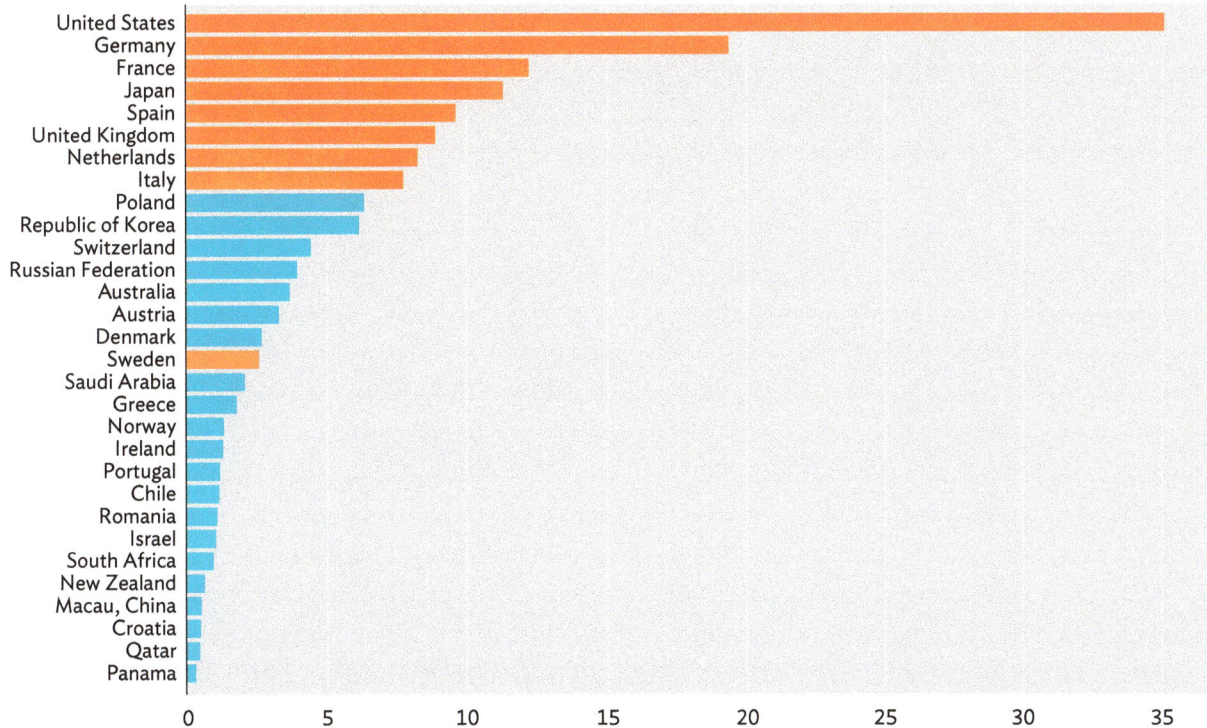

HS = harmonized system.

Note: HS 61 refers to "articles of apparel and clothing accessories, knitted or crocheted," while HS 62 refers to "articles of apparel and clothing accessories, not knitted or crocheted."

Sources: United Nations. Comtrade Database (accessed 20 November 2022); and Asian Development Bank estimates.

Chapter 6

DIGITALIZATION AND ECONOMIC TRANSFORMATION IN BANGLADESH

For developing economies like Bangladesh, exporting has been an important pathway toward economic diversification, rapid inclusive growth, job creation, and poverty reduction. Since the 1980s, Bangladesh has successfully moved away from agriculture to manufacturing, with its economic growth driven by the labor-intensive and export-oriented ready-made garments (RMG) manufacturing sector. The RMG industry accounts for about 20% of the country's gross domestic product (GDP), employing around 5 million workers, of which about 80% are women (Swazan and Das 2022). Much of the success of its RMG sector lies in the vast labor force pool, lower wages compared with other countries, suitable locations, and targeted export interventions by the Government of Bangladesh (Zaman 2021; Hasan et al. 2020; Swazan and Das 2022).

While the RMG sector will continue to be an important sector for inclusive economic growth in the economy, new developments and the evolving geopolitical and geoeconomic dynamics are challenging garments-led manufacturing economic growth in Bangladesh. First, average monthly incomes in Bangladesh's manufacturing sector have been on the rise, increasing by 3.1% in 2018 from 2013, while economies such as Ethiopia, Myanmar, and Cambodia are emerging as lower-cost locations (Gu, Nayyar, and Sharma 2021). Wages are expected to rise even further as Bangladesh graduates from its least-developed-country status. Second, the COVID-19 pandemic in 2020 bought an end to the already declining period of "hyper-globalization" in Bangladesh (Sattar and Ahmed 2021) (Figure 6.1). The financial year 2020 was showing an export decline of about 6.0% by March 2020, and then, as per news reports, the RMG sector was hit hard by the pandemic and the subsequent suspension of export orders from the United States (US) and Europe (Al Fattah 2020).

Third, the global manufacturing landscape has rapidly evolved with the rise of Industry 4.0 (or the fourth industrial revolution). Digital technologies, such as the Internet of Things, big data, machine learning, 3D printing, and robotics, are changing comparative advantages in the manufacturing sector, reducing the importance of lower wages in determining competitiveness (Hallward-Driemeier and Nayyar 2017). The accelerating digital development will affect the garments manufacturing sector in Bangladesh through both national and international pathways. National pathways include the effects of the adoption of automation and digital technologies within Bangladesh's garments manufacturing. For example, the adoption of management and exchange online platforms can improve the efficiency of garments firms in Bangladesh, while the adoption of modern computer numerical control lasers in the factories can reduce workers in the cutting tasks. International pathways include the effects through reconfiguring of garments global value chains (GVCs) as a result of digital adoption in manufacturing lead/buyer firms. For instance, the adoption of sewbots (fully automated sewing robots) for apparel manufacturing in

Figure 6.1: Bangladesh Export and Import Growth, 2015–2020
(%)

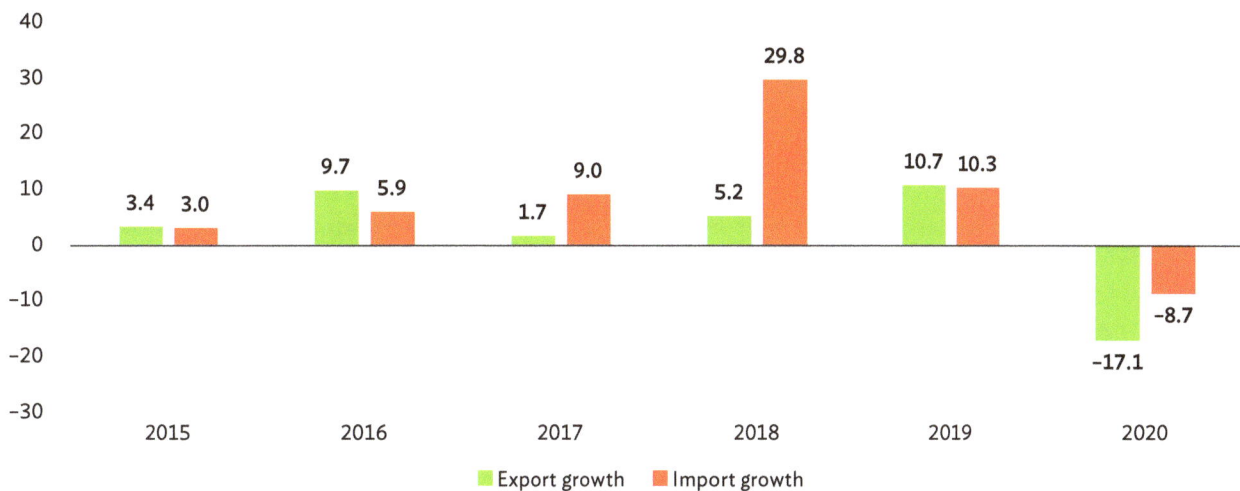

Source: Z. Sattar and Z. Ahmed. 2021. *Post-COVID19 Export Development Strategy for Bangladesh*. Bangladesh Trade Policy and Negotiation Capacity Building Support Project. London: ODI. http://pri-odi-tradenegotiaitons-capacitybuilding-taf2-moc.com/wp-content/uploads/2021/03/Export-Development-Strategy-Post-Covid-19.pdf.

the People's Republic of China (PRC), Europe and the US can lead to limited offshoring of future apparel manufacturing jobs to Bangladesh or even lead to increased re-shoring of apparel manufacturing jobs from Bangladesh. Evidence suggests that increased robot density in high-income countries is negatively associated with the growth rate of outbound foreign direct investment (FDI) from these countries to low-and middle-income countries (Hallward-Driemeier and Nayyar 2019).

As global pressures intensify, there is an urgent and critical need for Bangladesh to break its current pattern of economic transformation. There are important challenges in terms of lack of economic and export diversification, slow employment generation and high prevalence of the informal sector, but new opportunities lie in the digital economy and through a rapid growth of e-commerce in the economy. The next sections map Bangladesh's journey to economic transformation by examining sector relative productivity, the role of digitalization, and export diversification.

A.   Conceptualizing Economic Transformation

Economic transformation is defined as the continuous process of (i) moving labor and other resources from lower- to higher-productivity sectors (structural change) and (ii) raising within-sector productivity growth (McMillan, Rodrik, and Verduzco-Gallo 2014). This indicates that labor productivity growth can be decomposed into a between-sector component (structural change) and a within-sector component (Box 6.1).

Box 6.1: Decomposition of Labor Productivity Growth

This decomposition of labor productivity is expressed as:

$$\Delta P_t = \sum_{i=n} \theta_{i,t-k}\Delta p_{i,t} + \sum_{i=n} p_{i,t}\Delta \theta_{i,t}$$

where P_t refers to economy-wide productivity level, $P_{i,t}$ is sector labor productivity level, and $\theta_{i,t}$ is the share of employment in sector i. The Δ operator denotes the change in productivity or employment shares between t-k and t. The first term in the decomposition is the "within-sector" component of productivity growth, calculated as the weighted sum of productivity growth within individual sectors, with the weights equal to the employment share of each sector at the beginning of the time period. The second term is the structural change, calculated as the inner productivity levels (at the end of the time period), with changes in employment shares across sectors. When changes in employment shares are positively correlated with productivity levels, this term will be positive.

Source: M. McMillan, D. Rodrik, and Í. Verduzco-Gallo. 2014. Globalization, Structural Change, and Productivity Growth, with an Update on Africa. *World Development*. Elsevier. 63. pp.11–32.

Recent evidence indicates that structural change has played a substantial role in the productivity catchup of developing economies to the productivity of the US, especially in sectors more exposed to international trade (Duarte and Restuccia 2010). The manufacturing sector has been traditionally used by developing economies as a first step toward economic transformation and job creation. Since 1960, the tradability of manufacturing products has led to countries exhibiting unconditional convergence in labor productivity (Rodrik 2013). This implies that less developed economies eventually catch up with the productivity levels of developed economies in the manufacturing sector.

The rapid advancements in information and communication technology (ICT) in the 1990s enabled the fragmentation of production and made it viable to offshore manufacturing tasks and other business functions to different economies based on their comparative advantages (Grossman and Rossi-Hansberg 2008). Now, with the spread of digital technologies and rising "servification" of manufacturing, the boundaries across sectors have blurred. An advantage of the McMillan, Rodrik, and Verduzco-Gallo (2014) approach toward economic transformation is the inclusion of movement of workers not just across sectors but also across low- to high-productivity activities, which can combine agriculture, manufacturing, and services tasks. Within-sector productivity growth is attained through the following: (i) reallocation of resources from low- to high-productivity firms and farms within a given sector, and (ii) productivity improvements within existing firms or farms by moving into more efficient product lines.

Production lines within the same factory in Bangladesh's garments firms show a significant degree of variance, with productivity being two-thirds higher in the most efficient production line compared to the least efficient production line (Woodruff 2014). Increased productivity typically involves diversification in trade and production and higher value addition in export activities, especially in manufacturing. Additionally, evidence suggests that faster growth rates are associated with more complex production and export structures within economies. The Hidalgo et al. (2007) product space analysis can provide new insights into an economy's complexity and the type of products an economy can move into next given the country's current production and trade structure.

Digitalization has emerged as an important driver of economic transformation. While an implicit link between digitalization and structural change can be found in some studies (e.g., Rodrik 2018; Newfarmer, Page, and Tarp 2019), there are very few studies that provide an explicit conceptualization of digitalization as a driver of structural transformation, and even more limited is the empirical evidence on the same. A recent literature review (Matthess and Kunkel 2020) adopts an integrative perspective on structural change and digitalization, revealing that digitalization is affecting structural change through both direct and indirect channels (Figure 6.2). Direct channels include sector differences in digitalization, which leads to changes in the relative productivity of sectors and, therefore, prices. On an aggregate level, many studies report a positive correlation between the use of or access to digital technologies and the productivity growth of national economies. Banga and te Velde (2018), for example, analyze the impact of digitalization on manufacturing labor productivity using a cross-country panel and demonstrate that technological advancement, particularly Internet penetration, contributes to higher manufacturing labor productivity by 10% in all developing economies, but it is lower for low-income economies and Sub-Saharan Africa economies.

Indirect channels include the impact of digitalization on structural change through its effects on other drivers such as occupational structures, input–output linkages, and trade (Matthess and Kunkel 2020). Economic transformation is normally associated with export diversification, increased domestic value addition in exports, and upgrading in value chains. The rise of digital technologies and new business models is taking place in the context of globalization and fragmentation of production systems in GVCs. Digital technologies lower the cost of communication, coordination, transportation, and information procurement, which can facilitate trade (Hallward-Driemeier and Nayyar 2017); create new opportunities for micro, small, and medium enterprises; and lead to export expansion in low- and middle-income countries (Hjort and Poulsen 2019). Advanced digital technologies are therefore serving as powerful new tools for accelerating innovation and structural transformation (Andreoni and Roberts 2020; Sturgeon 2021).

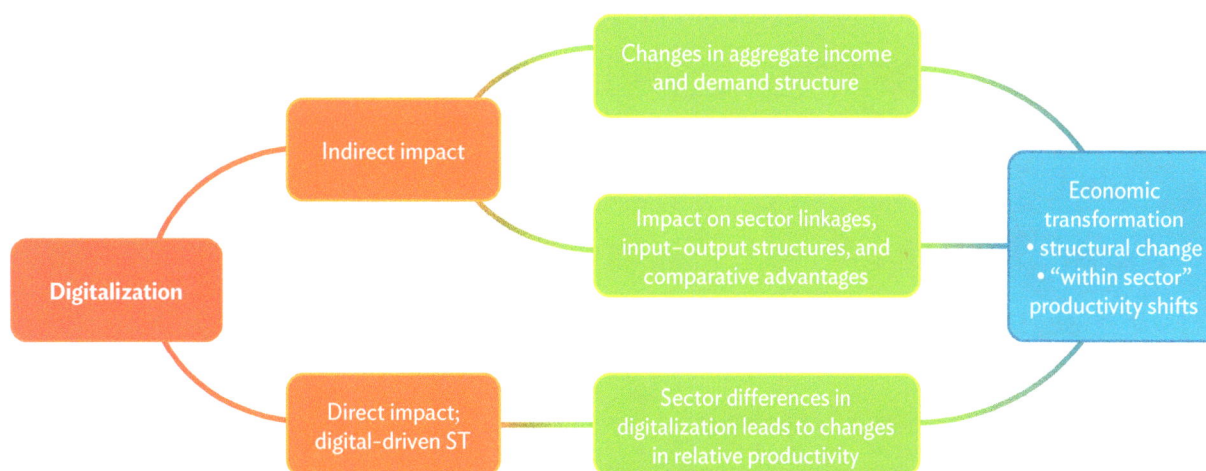

Figure 6.2: Digital-Led Economic Transformation

ST = structural transformation.
Source: Adapted from M. Matthess and S. Kunkel. 2020. Structural Change and Digitalization in Developing Countries: Conceptually Linking the Two Transformations. *Technology in Society*. 63. 101428. https://doi.org/10.1016/j.techsoc.2020.101428.

To emerging economies with a large micro, small, and medium enterprise-led informal sector, e-commerce, in particular, holds significant potential. The use of e-commerce provides opportunities for small-sized firms that have very limited capital base to reach customers in distant markets without the costs of establishment or the use of intermediaries (Broome 2016). There is some evidence of e-commerce enabling export diversification as well. While apparel remains the top "offline" category for exports in Bangladesh, it accounts for a smaller share of total purchase inquiries on Alibaba.com (ITC 2018). Only 47% of all purchase inquiries on Alibaba.com received by sellers from Bangladesh were related to apparel. A significant number of inquiries involved other products, including agriculture (6%), food and beverages (5%), and consumer electronics (5%).

B.   Bangladesh's Patterns of Structural Transformation

Industrial labor productivity in Bangladesh rose rapidly in 1990–1996, stagnated between 1996 and 2010, but rapidly increased post-2010 (Figure 6.3). There are significant productivity differentials across sectors, with industrial labor productivity in Bangladesh being higher than services and agriculture productivity in 2019. Between 2005 and 2010, structural change accounted for 0.47% of labor productivity growth but increased to 1.04% in 2015–2018 (Figure 6.4). This indicates that the structural change component of labor productivity growth has increased over time, and this change has been growth-enhancing. However, within-sector productivity growth continues to drive productivity growth in Bangladesh, consistent with findings in other countries (McMillan, Rodrik, and Verduzco-Gallo 2014)

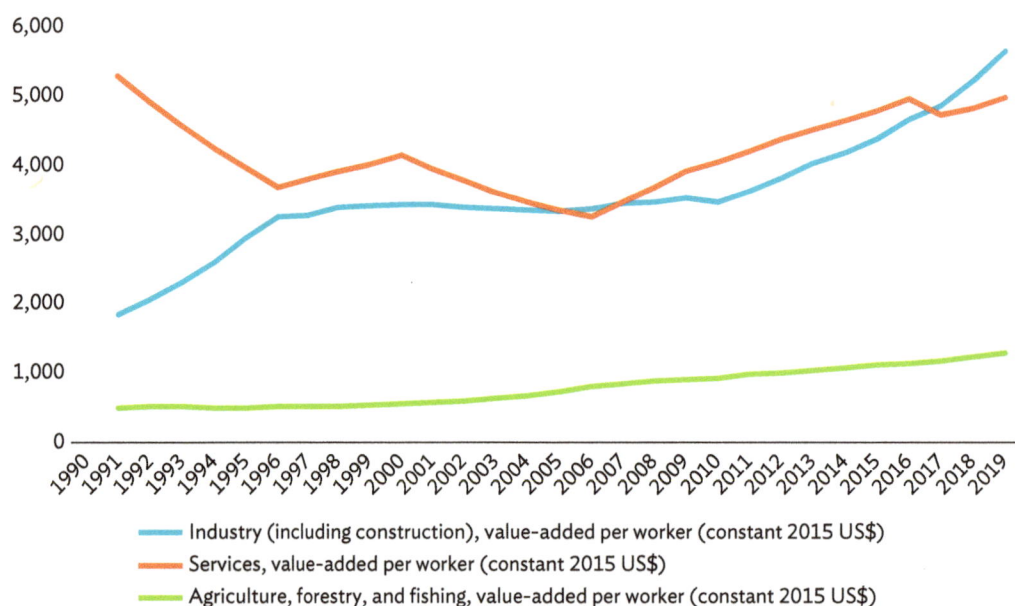

Figure 6.3: Bangladesh Sector Labor Productivity, 1990–2019

Industry (including construction), value-added per worker (constant 2015 US$)
Services, value-added per worker (constant 2015 US$)
Agriculture, forestry, and fishing, value-added per worker (constant 2015 US$)

Sources: World Bank. World Development Indicators (accessed 15 October 2022); and United Nations University World Institute for Development Economics Research. Economic Transformation Database (accessed 15 October 2022).

Figure 6.4: Bangladesh Labor Productivity Decomposition

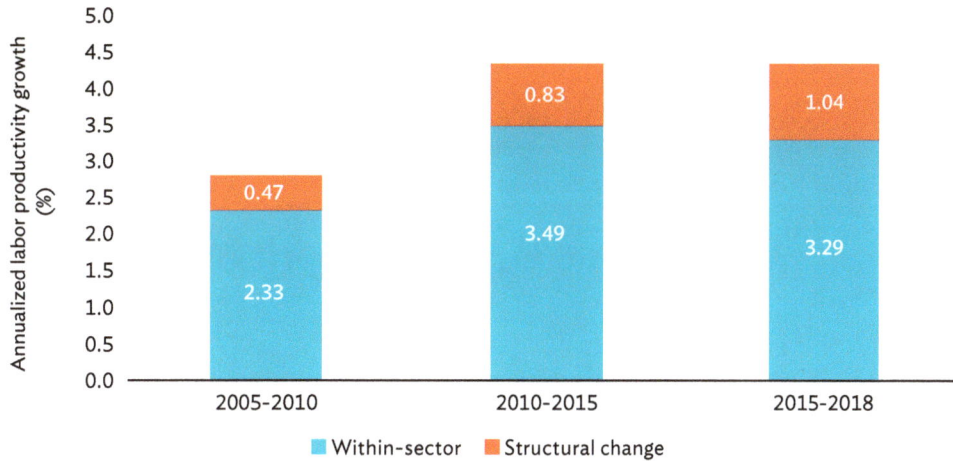

Note: Labor productivity decomposition into within-sector and structural change components follows the methodology specified in Box 1.
Sources: World Bank. World Development Indicators (accessed 15 October 2022); and United Nations University World Institute for Development Economics Research. Economic Transformation Database (accessed 15 October 2022).

Figure 6.5 and Figure 6.6 take a closer look at structural change in Bangladesh, distinguishing the manufacturing sector from the industrial sector. In 2010, the construction, mining, and utility sector was the most productive, followed by services, manufacturing, and agriculture. In the 5 years leading up to 2010, the employment share of manufacturing rose by 1.0 percentage point and construction rose by 1.5 percentage points, while the employment shares of agriculture and services declined. In contrast, between 2015 and 2018, both the agriculture and manufacturing employment shares declined, while that in services and construction increased.

Figure 6.5: Relative Labor Productivity in 2010 and Percentage-Point Change in Employment Share in 2005–2010

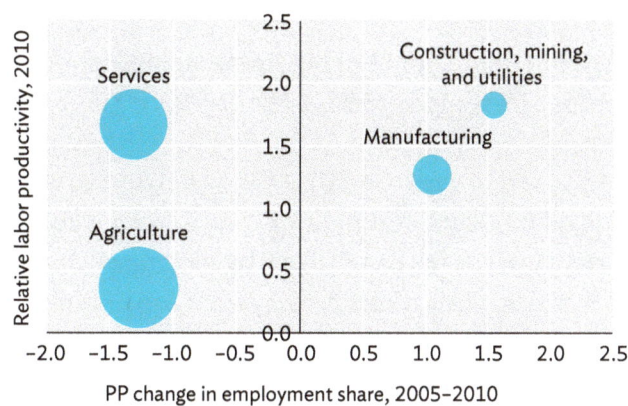

PP = percentage point.
Note: The size of the bubbles represents the number of persons employed in each sector in the later year of the period.
Sources: United Nations University World Institute for Development Economics Research. Economic Transformation Database (15 October 2022); and Asian Development Bank estimates.

Figure 6.6: Relative Labor Productivity in 2018 and Percentage-Point Change in Employment Share in 2015–2018

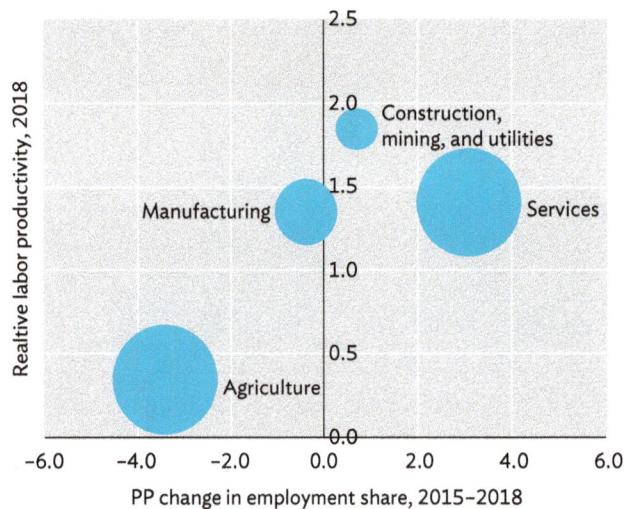

PP = percentage point.
Note: The size of the bubbles represents the number of persons employed in each sector in the later year of the period.
Sources: United Nations University World Institute for Development Economics Research. Economic Transformation Database (15 October 2022); and Asian Development Bank estimates.

Over the last 4 decades, economic growth in Bangladesh has brought important structural changes in the economy. The share of manufacturing grew from just 7% to 28%, and the share of services increased from 35% to more than 50% (Raihan and Khan 2020). The pattern of economic transformation has been heavily linked to trade in the RMG sector and subsequent job creation, with export diversification remaining an important challenge. Despite a high share of manufacturing exports in total merchandise exports, the export basket of Bangladesh remains concentrated in low complexity, low value-added goods. In 2020, Bangladesh's exports equaled approximately $39.6 billion, with the export basket being dominated by RMG goods and ICT services (Figure 6.7).

Bangladesh's 2020 rank on the Economic Complexity Index based on Harmonized System (HS) 1992 classification was 102nd, lower than its comparators Cambodia (92nd), Pakistan (89th), Viet Nam (61st), India (45th) and the PRC (20th) (Figure 6.8). Since 2005, Bangladesh has added only 10 products, and these products contributed to $2 per capita in 2020 (The Growth Lab at Harvard University n.d.). In comparison, Viet Nam added 44 products, contributing to $1,254 per capita in 2020. Viet Nam's transformation provides important lessons for Bangladesh; by targeting FDIs and regional production networks, Viet Nam managed to successfully diversify away from agriculture into textiles, followed by electronics and/or machinery manufacturing. Bangladesh can achieve manufacturing export diversification through a similar strategy of targeting investments in specific high-potential sectors and products. In this regard, Table 6.1 identifies the top 10 nontextile products (at 6-digit HS classification) where Bangladesh enjoys significant competitive advantage and therefore has strong export diversification potential. Both normalized and non-normalized values of the RCA index have been provided.

Figure 6.7: Bangladesh Economic Complexity, 2020

ICT = information and communication technology.
Note: Numbers are in percent of total exports.
Source: The Growth Lab at Harvard University. 2019. International Trade Data (HS, 92). V5. Harvard Dataverse (accessed 18 November 2022).

Figure 6.8: Economic Complexity Rankings, Bangladesh and Comparators, 1995–2020

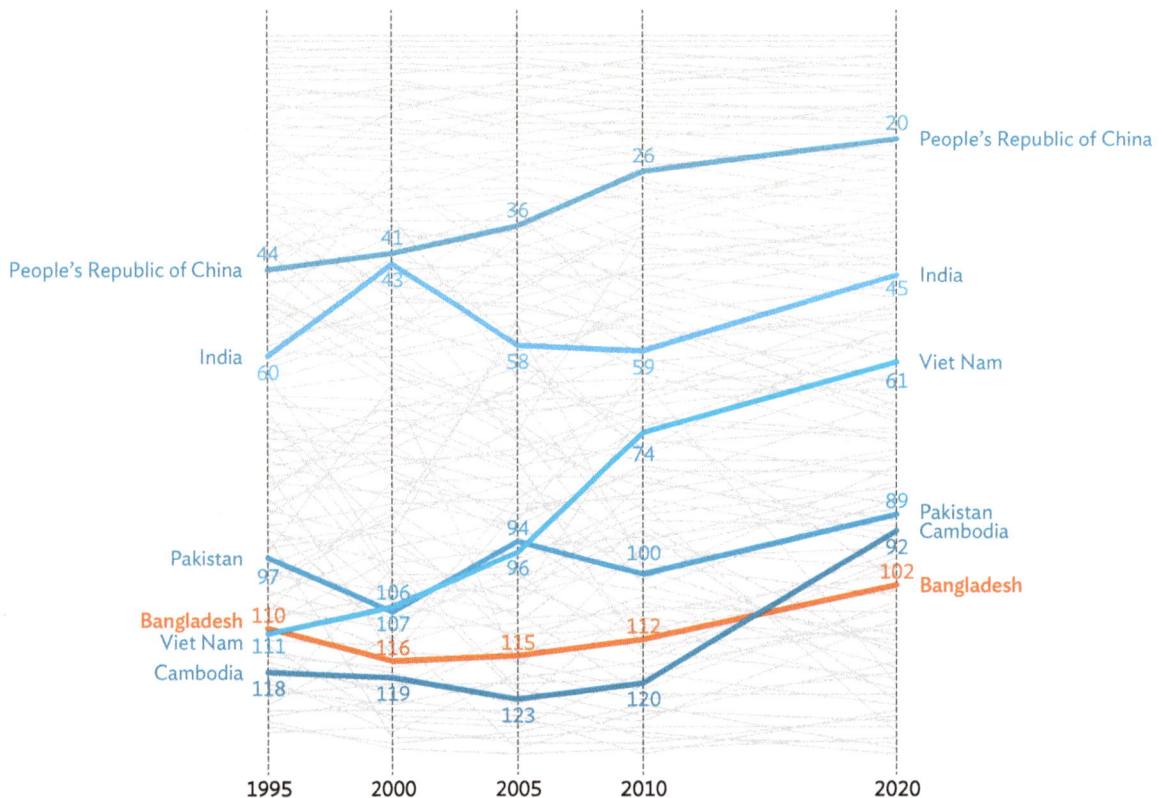

Note: Economic complexity index (ECI) rankings are based on the Harmonized System rev. 1992 classification. ECI ranks economies based on the diversity of exports an economy produces and their ubiquity, or the number of economies able to produce them (and those economies' complexity). **Source:** The Growth Lab at Harvard University. 2019. Growth Projections and Complexity Rankings. V3. Harvard Dataverse (accessed 18 November 2022).

Six of the top 10 competitive products in Table 6.1 belong to the leather and leather footwear sector, which has already been identified as a priority sector, given its growth, investment, and employment-creating potential (Razzaque et al. 2020). In the export product space, leather footwear products are closely linked to the RMG clusters, indicating that manufacturing countries that specialize in garments will find it easier to specialize in footwear as well. Bangladesh can use its design and productive capabilities gained in garments manufacturing to diversify into the closely related leather sector. Previous studies have also found that the quality of many of Bangladesh's leather products is better than that of its comparators (Razzaque et al. 2020). While the leather industry can potentially develop strong backward linkages with mostly locally sourced materials, access to finance and modern production technologies remain key challenges to the industry's growth (ADB 2018).

Table 6.1: Revealed Comparative Advantage of the Top 10 Products of Bangladesh, 2020

Sector	Product Code	Product Description (6-digit level, HS 2002 Classification)	BRCA	NRCA
Leather, leather products, and footwear	640391	Footwear; NES in heading no. 6403, covering the ankle, outer soles of rubber, plastics or composition leather, uppers of leather	10.4	0.165
Food, beverages, and tobacco	30613	Crustaceans; shrimps and prawns, frozen (whether in shell or not, whether or not cooked by steaming or by boiling in water)	7.2	0.160
Leather, leather products, and footwear	640399	Footwear; NES in heading no. 6403, not covering the ankle, outer soles of rubber, plastics or composition leather, uppers of leather	3.9	0.102
Food, beverages, and tobacco	151590	Vegetable fats and oils and their fractions; fixed, NES in heading no. 1515, whether or not refined, but not chemically modified	17.8	0.062
Leather, leather products, and footwear	640419	Footwear; other than sportswear, with outer soles of rubber or plastics and uppers of textile materials	3.0	0.061
Manufacturing, NEC; recycling	670419	False beards, eyebrows and eyelashes, switches and the like; of synthetic textile materials	38.4	0.046
Transport equipment	871200	Bicycles and other cycles; including delivery tricycles, not motorized	4.5	0.045
Leather, leather products, and footwear	640340	Footwear; with metal toe-cap, outer soles of rubber, plastics, leather or composition leather, uppers of leather	10.8	0.032
Leather, leather products, and footwear	640411	Sports footwear; tennis shoes, basketball shoes, gym shoes, training shoes and the like, with outer soles of rubber or plastics and uppers of textile materials	2.2	0.026
Leather, leather products, and footwear	410441	Tanned or crust hides and skins; bovine or equine, without hair on, in the dry state (crust), full grains, unsplit; grain splits	23.5	0.024

BRCA = Balassa-based revealed comparative advantage, NEC = not elsewhere classified, NRCA = normalized revealed comparative advantage. NES = not elsewhere specified.
Notes: Following Balassa (1965), a product's revealed comparative advantage (RCA) is measured as the share of the total exports of the commodity in the country's total exports, which is then divided by the share of world exports of the commodity in total world exports. The Balassa RCA indexes are normalized following the methodology of Yu, Cai, and Leung (2009), as summarized in Chapter 4, and multiplied by 10,000.
Sources: Centre d'Etudes Prospectives d'Informations Internationales (CEPII). BACI International Trade Database (accessed 21 July 2022); B. Balassa. 1965. Trade Liberalisation and "Revealed" Comparative Advantage. *The Manchester School.* 33 (2). pp. 99–123; and R. Yu, J. Cai, and P. S. Leung. 2009. The Normalized Revealed Comparative Advantage Index. *Annals of Regional Science.* 43 (1). pp. 267–282.

C.   Digital Development and Digital Trade in Bangladesh

1.   Digital Trade in Bangladesh

Bangladesh has made important progress on key digital development indicators. The percentage of the total population with access to the Internet as well as fixed broadband subscriptions per 100 people doubled in the period 2015–2021 (Table 6.2). However, as the table shows, Bangladesh continues to lag on key digital development indicators when compared with Sri Lanka and Viet Nam, including on total Internet penetration, fixed broadband access, and Internet bandwidth. This could explain why Bangladesh's global rank on the United Nations Conference on Trade and Development B2C E-Commerce Index for 2020 was 115th, lower than Sri Lank (91st) and Viet Nam (63rd) (UNCTAD 2021a). The e-Commerce Association of Bangladesh estimates that e-commerce contributions to Bangladesh's GDP are just 0.2% (Banga and Mendez-Parra 2021), with roughly 90% of e-commerce being business-to-consumer (B2C). The most prominent channel of B2C e-commerce in the country is through social media platforms, such as Facebook, also called "f-commerce." The slow adoption of e-commerce in the country could, in part, be explained by the high cost of data in the country and poor postal reliability, a key indicator of the B2C e-commerce index (Banga and Mendez-Parra 2021).

Table 6.2: Digital Development Indicators

Country	Fixed Broadband Subscriptions (per 100 inhabitants)		Individuals Using the Internet, Total (%)		International Bandwidth per Internet User (kbit/s)		E-Commerce Index (B2C)	
	2015	2021	2015	2021	2015	2021	Rank, 2020	Value, 2020
Bangladesh	3.1	6.0	12.9	25.0	9,911	59,369	115	33.3
Cambodia	0.5	2.0	18.0	52.0	19,097	...	117	31.1
Pakistan	0.8	1.3	11.0	25.0	17,376	55,774	116	32.5
Sri Lanka	2.9	11.9	12.1	35.0	39,701	47,028	91	47.8
Viet Nam	8.3	19.8	45.0	70.3	40,441	204,886	63	61.6

... = data not available, B2C = business-to-consumer, kbit/s = kilobit per second.
Notes: Data for 2020 is used when data for 2021 is missing. The B2C E-Commerce Index of the United Nations Conference on Trade and Development is compiled from information on the Internet and account penetration, secure Internet servers, and postal reliability.
Source: International Telecommunication Union. ICT Digital Development Dashboard (accessed 5 November 2022).

In terms of digital services trade, the share of digitally deliverable services (DDS) exports in total services trade has remained consistently higher than the share of DDS imports in 2005–2021 (Figure 6.9). Both ICT and DDS export shares in total services rapidly increased in 2005–2011 but declined post-2011. The effects of the pandemic are reflected in the upturn of ICT services exports from 2020 to 2021.

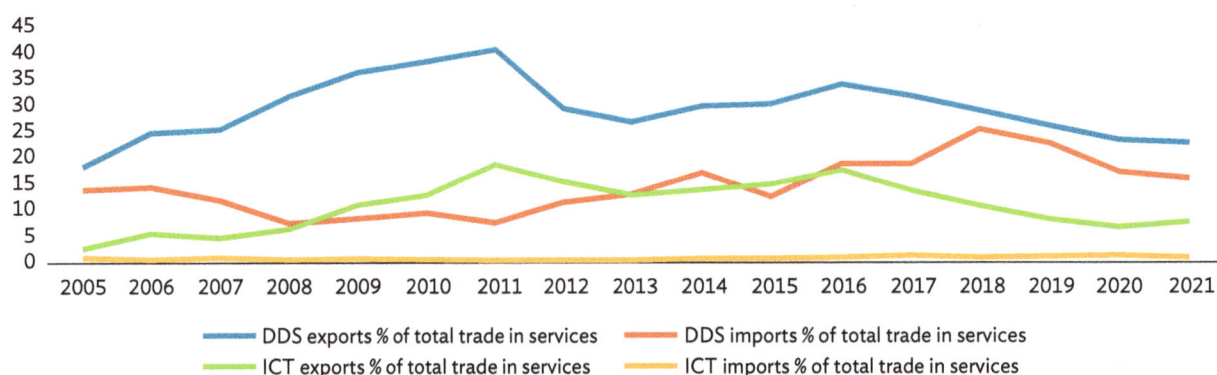

Figure 6.9: Bangladesh Digitally Deliverable Services, 2005–2021

DDS = digitally deliverable services, ICT = information and communication technology.
Source: United Nations Conference on Trade and Development. UNCTADstat (accessed 10 November 2022).

Services can be supplied through four modes: cross-border supply of ICT services or online delivery (Mode 1), consumption of ICT services abroad (Mode 2), supply of ICT services through FDI or foreign affiliates (Mode 3), and supply of services through movements of natural persons across borders (Mode 4). While the majority of ICT exports in Bangladesh are supplied online through Mode 1, the share of Mode 1 services has declined from 2010 to 2015 to 2017 (Figure 6.10). In contrast, 97.0% of ICT services are imported into Bangladesh through foreign affiliates (Mode 3) and 2.65% through cross-border online channels, such as digital marketplaces (Figure 6.11).

Figure 6.10: Bangladesh Information and Communication Technology Services Exports, 2005–2017
(%)

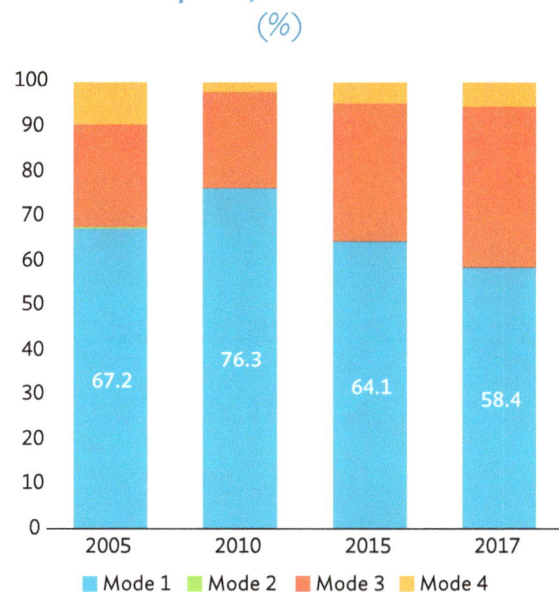

Notes: Mode 1 refers to cross-border supply of information and communication technology (ICT) services or online delivery. Mode 2 refers to consumption of ICT services abroad. Mode 3 refers to supply of ICT services through foreign direct investments or foreign affiliates. Mode 4 refers to supply of services through movements of natural persons across borders.
Sources: United Nations Conference on Trade and Development. UNCTADstat (accessed 10 November 2022); and World Trade Organization. 2019. Trade in Services Data by Mode of Supply (TiSMOS) (accessed 10 November 2022).

Figure 6.11: Bangladesh Information and Communication Technology Services Imports, 2017
(%)

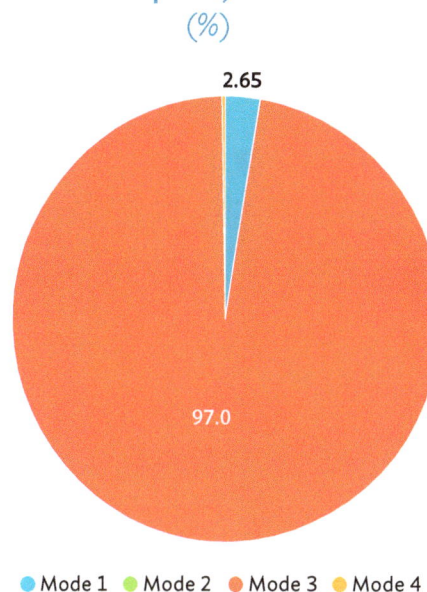

Notes: Mode 1 refers to cross-border supply of information and communication technology (ICT) services or online delivery. Mode 2 refers to consumption of ICT services abroad. Mode 3 refers to supply of ICT services through foreign direct investments or foreign affiliates. Mode 4 refers to supply of services through movements of natural persons across borders.
Sources: United Nations Conference on Trade and Development. UNCTADstat (accessed 10 November 2022); and World Trade Organization. 2019. Trade in Services Data by Mode of Supply (TiSMOS) (accessed 10 November 2022).

2.   Digitalization of the Economy and Subsectors

ADB (2021a) proposes a framework for calculating digital GDP using backward and forward linkages of the digital sectors, the value-added by the other sectors to the fixed investment demand of the digital sectors, and a double-counting term (Box 6.2). Digital GDP typically ranges from 2.0% to 9.0% of the total GDP across countries (ADB 2021a). Using this framework, Figure 6.12 notes that, in 2021, Bangladesh's digital GDP was just 2.6% of its total GDP. Moreover, digital GDP has been on a declining trend in Bangladesh, having decreased from 2.8% in 2016. This declining share of the digital economy in GDP was also observed by ADB (2021a) for other economies, except Canada, India, the Republic of Korea, Malaysia, and the US. It is noted that ADB's supply–use tables and national input–output tables used for these calculations are based on current prices. The derived measures, therefore, are not able to account for the drop-in prices of digital consumer products over time, cautioning temporal inferences on digital GDP.

Box 6.2: ADB's Proposed Framework for the Calculation of Digital Gross Domestic Product

The digital gross domestic product (GDP) equation is given as

$$\text{GDP}_{\text{digital}} = \mathbf{i}^{\text{T}}\hat{\mathbf{v}}\mathbf{B}\hat{\mathbf{y}}\boldsymbol{\varepsilon}_1 + \mathbf{i}^{\text{T}}(\hat{\mathbf{v}}\mathbf{B}\hat{\mathbf{y}})^{\text{T}}\boldsymbol{\varepsilon}_1 - [\text{diag}(\hat{\mathbf{v}}\mathbf{B}\hat{\mathbf{y}})]^{\text{T}}\boldsymbol{\varepsilon}_1 + (\mathbf{i} - \boldsymbol{\varepsilon}_1)^{\text{T}}\hat{\mathbf{v}}\mathbf{B}\hat{\mathbf{y}}\hat{\mathbf{r}}\boldsymbol{\varepsilon}_2$$

where the first term of the equation refers to backward linkages or the total value embedded in final demand of core digital products; the second term refers to forward linkages, or the total value-added by core digital sectors to the rest of the economy; the third term refers to a double-counting component, which is subtracted; the fourth term refers to the value-added contribution of the other sectors to the fixed investment demand of the core digital sectors.

Source: Asian Development Bank. 2021. *Capturing the Digital Economy: A Proposed Measurement Framework and Its Applications.* A Special Supplement to *Key Indicators for Asia and the Pacific 2021.* Manila. https://www.adb.org/sites/default/files/publication/722366/capturing-digital-economy-measurement-framework.pdf.

Figure 6.12: Bangladesh Digital GDP as a Percentage of Total GDP, 2016–2021

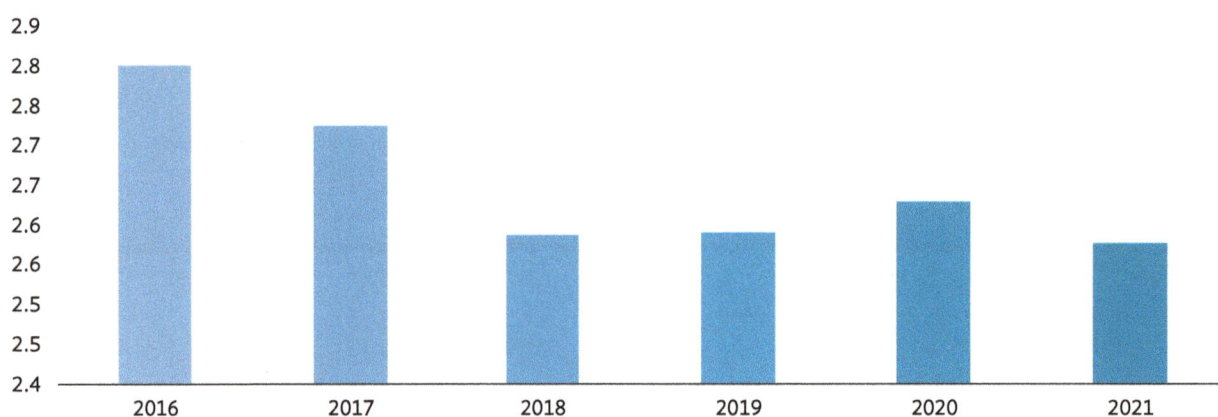

GDP = gross domestic product.
Note: See Box 6.2 for the methodology for calculating Digital GDP.
Source: Asian Development Bank. 2021. Multiregional Input–Output Tables (2016–2021).

The adoption of digital technologies and automation varies significantly across sectors. The digitalization rate of a sector in Bangladesh can be estimated based on the structure of inputs using the sector's production. Measuring the value-added by domestic "digital industries" into Sector X as a share of the total value-added by all sectors into Sector X is a good proxy of the digitalization rate of Sector X (ADB 2021a). Using this approach, Table 6.3 presents the digitalization rates across sectors in Bangladesh in the year 2021. Like other Asian economies, Bangladesh's sector digitalization rate is highest for computer and information services; telecommunications; and computer, electronic, and optical equipment. This is not surprising since these sectors are identified as the digital industries supplying digital inputs to the economy. The other sectors of Bangladesh that fare relatively better in digitalization include air transport, coke and refined petroleum, electrical machinery and apparatus, pulp and paper products, and rubber and plastic products.

It can be noted that the Indian economy is more diversified in terms of digitalized sectors as opposed to the rest of the Asian economies considered. Interestingly, at 0.95%, the digitalization rate of the textiles and textile products sector in Bangladesh is higher than its comparators, Maldives, Pakistan, and Sri Lanka, but significantly lower than India (3.28%). The digitalization rate of Bangladesh's leather and leather products sector is lower than that of India and Pakistan.

Table 6.3: Sector Digitalization Rates, 2021

Sector	India	Bangladesh	Maldives	Pakistan	Sri Lanka
Digital Industries					
Computer services, information	85.38	82.51	89.46	85.79	71.32
Telecommunications	69.42	76.79	81.49	62.31	65.42
Computer, electronic, and optical equipment	56.89	56.31	0.00	57.47	67.14
Nondigital Industries					
Air transport	11.63	3.92	11.64	0.86	1.27
Electrical machinery and apparatus	11.23	4.55	0.00	0.66	0.42
Other supporting and auxiliary transport activities	8.19	1.07	0.19	0.49	0.29
Renting of machinery and equipment, other business activities	5.60	0.51	1.21	0.76	0.92
Community, social, and personal services	5.20	0.51	0.57	0.88	0.98
Manufacturing, NEC; recycling	5.04	0.98	1.01	0.43	0.25
Water transport	4.93	0.71	3.26	0.67	0.35
Financial intermediation	4.62	1.32	0.51	1.21	0.67
Machinery, NEC	3.62	1.54	0.00	0.44	0.44
Transport equipment	3.32	1.54	1.42	0.34	0.29
Textiles and textile products	3.28	0.95	0.32	0.28	0.38
Pulp, paper, paper products, printing, and publishing	2.97	2.84	0.76	1.77	0.31
Leather, leather products, and footwear	2.76	0.58	0.00	1.06	0.36
Sale, maintenance, and repair of motor vehicles and motorcycles	2.14	0.16	2.94	0.36	0.36
Wholesale trade and commission trade	2.14	0.28	0.44	0.12	0.25
Retail trade; repairs	2.14	0.23	0.16	0.23	0.41
Food, beverages, and tobacco	2.09	0.69	2.73	0.14	0.15
Chemicals and chemical products	2.02	2.25	0.00	2.40	0.50
Health and social work	2.01	0.38	0.47	0.63	0.03
Rubber and plastics	1.76	2.48	0.00	0.81	0.12
Mining and quarrying	1.59	0.30	0.00	1.27	0.20
Wood and products of wood and cork	1.57	1.62	0.40	0.45	0.32
Other nonmetallic minerals	1.52	0.83	0.85	0.61	0.30
Construction	1.51	0.84	2.37	0.36	0.17
Education	1.39	0.38	0.71	0.49	0.02
Basic metals and fabricated metal	1.20	2.08	1.38	0.64	0.23
Electricity, gas, and water supply	1.19	2.02	2.04	0.72	0.99

continued on next page.

Table 6.3 *continued*.

Sector	India	Bangladesh	Maldives	Pakistan	Sri Lanka
Hotels and restaurants	1.10	0.67	2.80	1.45	0.15
Coke, refined petroleum, and nuclear fuel	1.01	3.19	0.00	0.48	0.17
Inland transport	0.93	0.54	0.28	0.86	0.29
Real estate activities	0.49	0.15	0.35	0.17	0.26
Agriculture, hunting, forestry, fishing	0.25	0.18	2.32	0.12	0.22
Postal	0.00	1.01	7.57	3.06	1.50
Public administration and defense	0.00	0.34	0.76	1.06	0.14
Private households with employed persons	...	...	...	...	0

... = data not available, NEC= not elsewhere classified.
Notes: Digital sectors include telecommunication; computer and information services; and computer, electronic, and optical apparatus. The digitalization rate is calculated as the share of domestic digital industries' value-added flows into Sector X over all value-added inputs flowing into Sector X (i.e., total backward linkage of Sector X). It shows how digital-intensive a sector's production is based on the structure of inputs used in its production. The digital foreign value-added into a sector's exports could be calculated using the Asian Development Bank Multiregional Input–Output Tables.
Sources: Asian Development Bank (ADB). 2021. Multiregional Input–Output Tables (2021); and ADB estimates.

D.   Digitalization and Economic Transformation in Bangladesh: Firm-Level Evidence

Firm-level studies analyzing the impact of digitalization on economic transformation have focused on different outcomes, including firm productivity, product and/or export sophistication and export intensity. For Indian firms, Banga (2022) finds that building digital capabilities significantly boosts the product sophistication in manufacturing GVCs, enabling product upgrading of supplier firms. Also focusing on India, Banga and Banga (2020) find that a rising share of digital assets in overall plant and machinery assets increases firm-level export intensity. For South African manufacturing micro and small enterprises, Gaglio, Kraemer-Mbula and Lorenz (2022) find a positive and significant impact of digital communication technologies on innovation and through that labor productivity. Similarly, for Cambodian firms, Hing, Thangavelu and Kong (2023) find a positive impact of technology on innovation and productivity.

For Bangladesh, the World Bank Enterprise Surveys (WBES) of 2007, 2011 and 2013 provide important information on the digitalization and GVC status of manufacturing firms. From this panel of firms, it is noted that roughly 54.0% of Bangladeshi manufacturing firms are using email to communicate with clients, while 34.7% of firms are using emails for communications in addition to having a web presence. Around 23.4% of the manufacturing firms in the panel are classified as GVC firms, i.e., firms that are simultaneously importing and exporting intermediate and final goods. Interestingly, 66.5% of GVC firms have a website as compared to only 2.5% of non-GVC firms.

Figure 6.13 notes that there is significant heterogeneity in the share of digitalized firms and GVC firms across industries in the panel. Almost 85.0% of firms in garments manufacturing are using emails to communicate with clients, and 58.6% are engaged in a GVC; whereas, in food processing, 27.3% of firms are using emails and 1.9% are in a GVC. The average export intensity is the highest in garments manufacturing firms (80.0%), followed by textiles (51.9%), leather (36.2%), and plastics and paper products (26.3%). While the chemicals, metals, and mineral sector has a low share of GVC firms, it fares well in terms of share of digitalized firms. More than 40% of the firms in the sector have a web presence, and almost 60% use emails to communicate with their clients.

Figure 6.13: Bangladesh Manufacturing Firms Panel, World Bank Enterprise Surveys

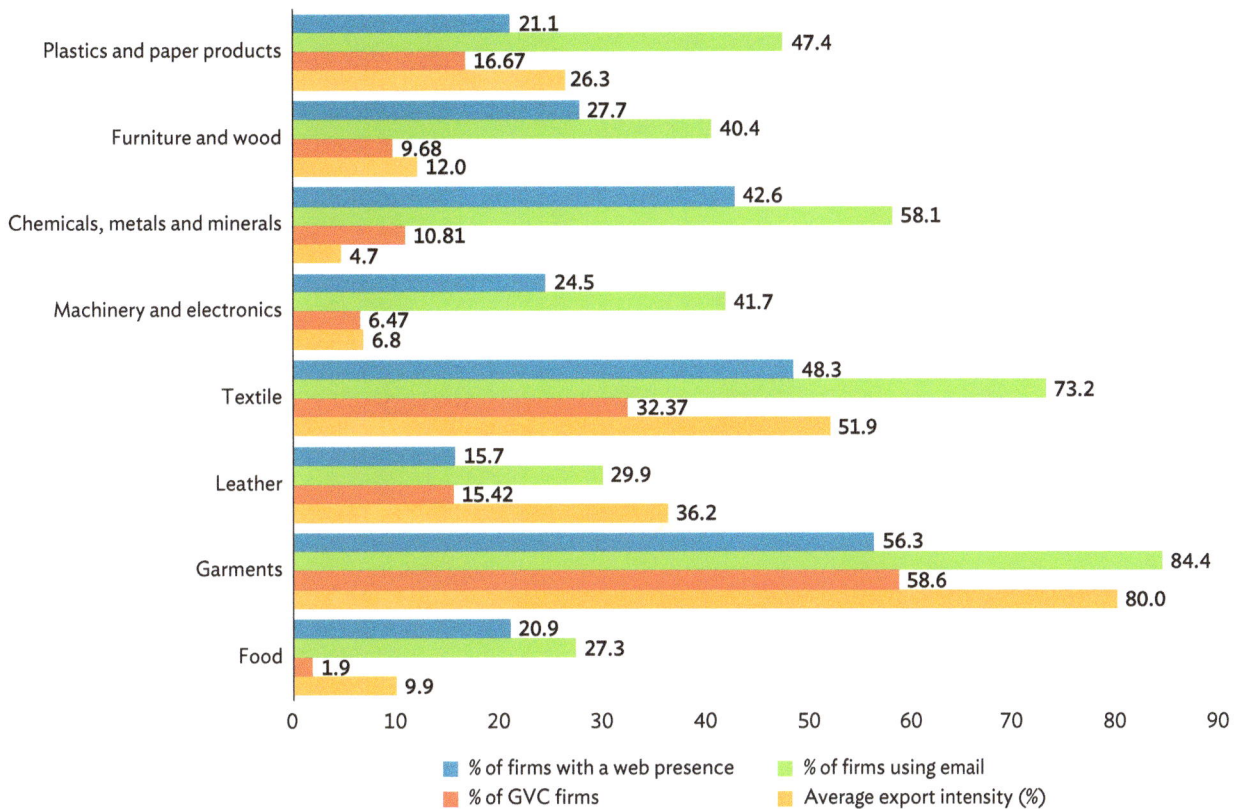

Sector	% of firms with a web presence	% of firms using email	% of GVC firms	Average export intensity (%)
Plastics and paper products	21.1	47.4	16.67	26.3
Furniture and wood	27.7	40.4	9.68	12.0
Chemicals, metals and minerals	42.6	58.1	10.81	4.7
Machinery and electronics	24.5	41.7	6.47	6.8
Textile	48.3	73.2	32.37	51.9
Leather	15.7	29.9	15.42	36.2
Garments	56.3	84.4	58.6	80.0
Food	20.9	27.3	1.9	9.9

GVC = global value chain.
Note: GVC firms are identified as two-way traders.
Source: World Bank Enterprise Surveys, 2007, 2011, 2013 panel, Bangladesh (accessed 5 October 2022).

The average TFP and export intensity in the panel is found to be higher for digitalized Bangladesh manufacturing firms compared to non-digitalized firms, and this difference is statistically significant at 1.0% (Figure 6.14 and Figure 6.15). This potentially indicates a positive correlation between digitalization and economic transformation in Bangladesh. It is critical, however, to take a closer look at the type of digital technologies being deployed in Bangladeshi firms as compared with its comparators in today's age. The latest firm-level technology adoption survey conducted by the World Bank reveals that firms in Viet Nam are more advanced than Bangladesh firms in the adoption of both general-purpose informational technologies and sector-specific production technologies across most manufacturing industries (Gu, Nayyar, and Sharma 2021). However, Viet Nam is just one technology level ahead of Bangladesh. In sector-specific technology in the garments industry, Bangladesh firms are at par with firms in Viet Nam and, in fact, more advanced than firms in Viet Nam in the pharmaceutical industry (Gu, Nayyar, and Sharma 2021). Interestingly, the survey finds Bangladesh to be particularly advanced in the use of more sophisticated sewing machines than Viet Nam, potentially explained by its large insertions in apparel manufacturing GVCs. Even incremental improvements in technology, particularly the use of technologies for general business functions such as payments and sales, could bring Bangladesh on par with its peers in manufacturing.

Figure 6.14: Bangladesh Mean Total Factor Productivity of Manufacturing Firms

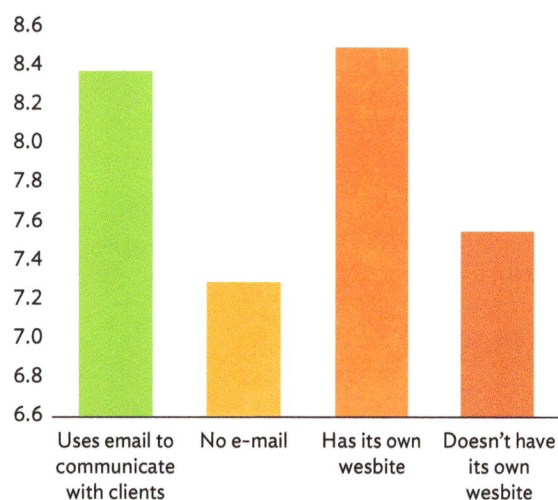

Note: Differences are significant at 1.0%. TFP is estimated using the Levinsohn-Petrin approach, which uses data on material inputs to control for unobserved productivity shocks.
Sources: World Bank Enterprise Surveys, 2007, 2011, 2013 panel, Bangladesh (accessed 5 October 2022).

Figure 6.15: Bangladesh Mean Export Intensity of Manufacturing Firms

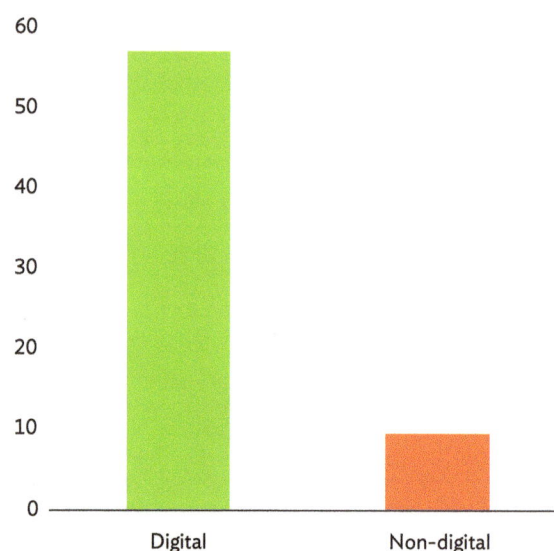

Note: Differences are significant at 1.0%.
Sources: World Bank Enterprise Surveys, 2007, 2011, 2013 panel, Bangladesh (accessed 5 October 2022).

E. Key Findings and Policy Recommendations

A key finding of this chapter is that the within-sector component of labor productivity growth is driving economic transformation in Bangladesh, but the structural change component has been increasing and growth-enhancing. Bangladesh's export basket, however, remains limited to low complexity, low value-added goods, indicating the lack of export diversification as a key challenge to economic transformation. Viet Nam's example shows how an economy can successfully transform by targeting FDI inflows to increase its GVC exports (Choi et al. 2021). It leveraged FDI and regional production networks to successfully diversify away from agriculture into textiles, followed by electronics and/or machinery manufacturing. This offers important lessons for Bangladesh to attract FDI into (i) manufacturing sectors other than apparels where it enjoys competitive advantage, such as leather and leather product sectors; and (ii) ICT and digital services. However, data suggests that the textile and wearing apparel accounted for about 18.5% of total FDI stock in Bangladesh, and 25.2% of FDI inflows in 2022, compared with 1.7% of total FDI stock and 3.0% of FDI inflows of the leather and leather products sectors (Figure 6.16). Similarly, telecommunications accounted for 5.2% of gross FDI, and computer software and IT services accounted for less than 1.0%. FDI inflows into the ICT sector are also heavily concentrated, with just five countries—Norway (59.6%), Malaysia (21.2%), Singapore (4.3%), the US (3.8%), and Japan (1.3%)—accounting for about 90.0% of total FDI inflows in 2022 (Figure 6.17).

Figure 6.16: Bangladesh Sector Share of Foreign Direct Investment, 2022
(%)

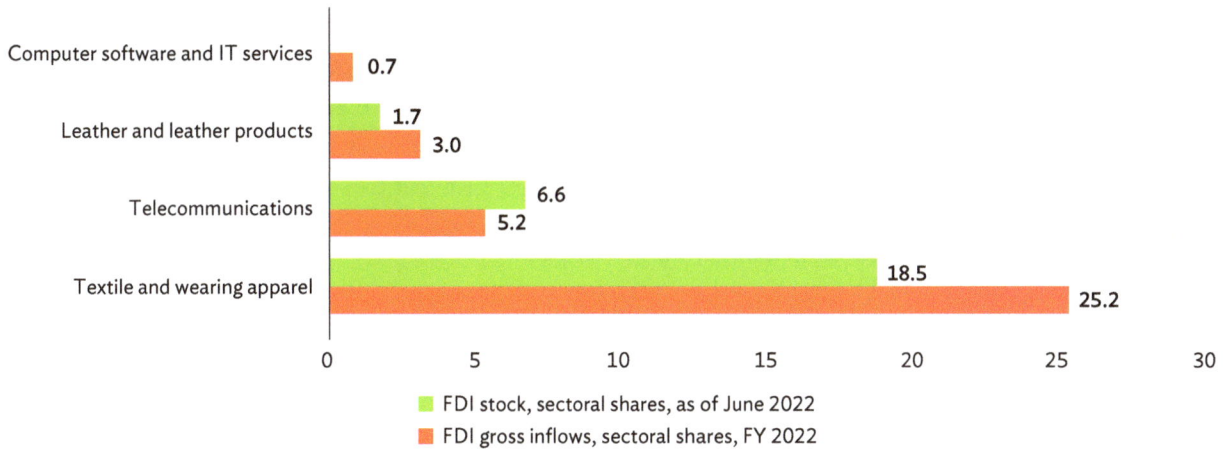

Sector	FDI stock, sectoral shares, as of June 2022	FDI gross inflows, sectoral shares, FY 2022
Computer software and IT services		0.7
Leather and leather products	1.7	3.0
Telecommunications	6.6	5.2
Textile and wearing apparel	18.5	25.2

■ FDI stock, sectoral shares, as of June 2022
■ FDI gross inflows, sectoral shares, FY 2022

FDI = foreign direct investment, FY = fiscal year, IT = information technology.
Source: Bangladesh Bank, Statistics Department. 2022. Foreign Investment and External Debt Management Cell (accessed 5 October 2022).

Figure 6.17: Bangladesh Origin of Foreign Direct Investment Inflows into the ICT Sector, 2022
(%)

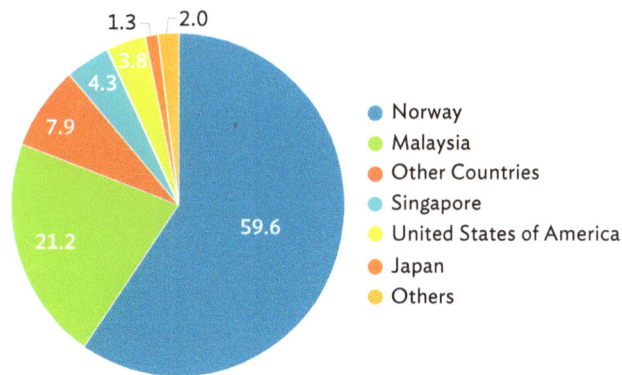

Norway	59.6
Malaysia	21.2
Other Countries	7.9
Singapore	4.3
United States of America	3.8
Japan	1.3
Others	2.0

ICT = information and communication technology.
Source: Bangladesh Bank, Statistics Department. 2022. Foreign Investment and External Debt Management Cell (accessed 5 October 2022).

Another key finding of the chapter is that there is much potential for a digital-led economic transformation in the country. Digitalized manufacturing firms in Bangladesh are found to have higher export intensity and productivity than non-digitalized manufacturing firms. However, the scope of digital-led transformation is narrowing due to a significant and widening digital divide between Bangladesh and its comparators. For instance, the gap in fixed broadband subscriptions rates between Viet Nam and Bangladesh was 13.8 percentage points in 2021, up from 5.2 percentage points in 2015. The share of digital GDP in the economy and the share of ICT exports supplied through Mode 1 (online channels) have also been on a declining trend in Bangladesh, indicating the urgent need for investments in digitalization.

In particular, Bangladesh needs to leverage digital technologies to enable export diversification in targeted manufacturing sectors, such as the leather, leather products, and footwear sector, where Bangladesh enjoys strong competitive advantage. However, the lack of access to modern technologies and finance continues to plague the sector, with Bangladesh ranking lower than both India and Pakistan in terms of the digitalization of the leather sector. Studies have also shown that Bangladesh is particularly more advanced in the use of more sophisticated sewing machines than Viet Nam, potentially explained by its large insertions in apparel manufacturing GVCs (Gu, Nayyar, and Sharma 2021). Policies that even incrementally improve technologies in the apparel manufacturing sector can bring Bangladesh on par with its peers in manufacturing.

Investment in digitalization needs to be supported with improvements in overall infrastructure that can facilitate the movement of goods and services within and across borders. The 2018 logistic performance index dataset of the World Bank shows that Bangladesh ranks 100th out of 160 economies in terms of the infrastructure dimension of the overall logistic performance index, suggesting the urgent need to improve infrastructure to facilitate trade. Human capital formation is also essential in building the skills needed for new manufacturing sectors as well as for coping with emerging technological advances and innovation in manufacturing. While Bangladesh has made gains in improving education in the economy, data suggests the need to further enhance education programs to reach majority of Bangladeshi workers. Latest data from the ILOSTAT database shows that, as of 2017, 35.5% of the working-age population received less than basic education and another 34.5% received only basic education.

Chapter 7

CONCLUSION

Bangladesh's Vision 2041 envisions an eradication of extreme poverty and a transition to upper-middle-income country status by 2031, and near-zero poverty and achievement of high-income country status by 2041 (Bangladesh Planning Commission 2020). Among the strategies of the Government of Bangladesh to realize its Vision 2041 is maintaining a sustainable balance of payments through export-oriented manufacturing expansion led by the ready-made garments (RMG) sector and diversification to other export products. As noted by the Bangladesh Planning Commission (2020), achieving its Vision 2041 will be largely driven by a competitive export sector.

A recurrent finding of the analyses in this report is the clear dominance of the textiles and textile products sector in exports production and global value chain (GVC) participation, leading to low export diversification. For Bangladesh, the textiles and textile products sector shows low forward and backward agglomeration, suggesting low value-added capture in the domestic economy and a limited role for domestic sectors in supporting domestic production in the sector. Chapters 5 and 6 also pointed out that such concentration in the textiles and textile products sector poses some risks to the economy, especially with the economy's graduation to lower-middle-income status, rising wages, and evolving global dynamics. Thus, diversification into the other sectors to supplement RMG manufacturing will be important in the economy's thrust to promote export-led growth. One way that Bangladesh can diversify its exports is by increasing participation in GVCs. This would allow the economy to specialize in certain tasks within value chains without needing to make heavy investments in building whole chains locally.

Analysis of revealed comparative advantage (RCA) shows that in 2021, Bangladesh had RCA in five other sectors: (i) post and telecommunications; (ii) leather, leather products, and footwear; (iii) public administration and defense; compulsory social work; (iv) construction; and (v) manufacturing, not elsewhere classified (NEC). These are sectors that Bangladesh can support in their journey toward realizing its Vision 2041. The GVC, competitiveness, and agglomeration indicators for these sectors and the textiles and textile products sector are summarized in Table 7.1. Sectors where Bangladesh has RCA have varying degrees of GVC participation and agglomeration profiles, but all of them are relatively downstream in terms of position.

Table 7.1: Bangladesh Revealed Comparative Advantage Sectors and Their Global Value Chain and Agglomeration Indicators, 2021

Sector	NRCA using Value-Added Exports	GVC Participation		Average GVC Length			Agglomeration	
		Trade-based Forward	Trade-based Backward	Forward	Backward	GVC Position	Forward	Backward
Textiles and textile products	6.41	0.01	0.25	3.55	4.46	0.80	0.71	0.60
Post and telecommunications	0.84	0.15	0.06	3.29	4.21	0.78	0.54	0.65
Leather, leather products and footwear	0.31	0.07	0.11	3.65	4.60	0.79	1.38	1.28
Public administration and defence; compulsory social work	0.32	0.21	0.06	3.64	4.40	0.83	0.96	1.01
Construction	0.22	0.15	0.18	3.77	4.47	0.84	1.01	0.99
Manufacturing, NEC; recycling	0.04	0.09	0.14	3.70	4.56	0.81	1.69	1.90

GVC = global value chain, NEC = not elsewhere classified, NRCA = normalized revealed comparative advantage.
Note: NRCA indexes are multiplied by 10,000. Numbers may not add up due to rounding. GVC position is the ratio between the average forward GVC length and the average backward GVC length.
Sources: Asian Development Bank (ADB). 2021. *Key Indicators for Asia and the Pacific 2021*. Manila; ADB. Multiregional Input–Output Database (accessed 14 July 2022); B. Balassa. 1965. Trade Liberalisation and "Revealed" Comparative Advantage. *The Manchester School*. 33 (2). pp. 99–123; K. V. Baris, M. C. R. Crisostomo, K. A. V. Garay, C. R. J. Jabagat, M. J. Mariasingham, and E. M. T. Mores. 2022. Measuring Localization in the Age of Economic Globalization. *ADB Economics Working Paper Series*. No. 647. Manila: ADB; Z. Wang, S. Wei, X. Yu, and K. Zhu. 2017. Measures of Participation in Global Value Chains and Global Business Cycles. *NBER Working Paper*. No. 23222. Cambridge, MA: National Bureau of Economic Research (NBER); Z. Wang, S. Wei, X. Yu, and K. Zhu. 2017. Characterizing Global Value Chains: Production Length and Upstreamness. *NBER Working Paper*. No. 23261. Cambridge, MA: NBER; R. Yu, J. Cai, and P. S. Leung. 2009. The Normalized Revealed Comparative Advantage Index. *Annals of Regional Science*. 43 (1). pp. 267–282; and ADB estimates.

Chapter 6 also laid out non-agriculture and non-textile products where Bangladesh has shown competitiveness in 2020 (Table 6.1). Many of these products fall under the leather, leather products, and footwear sector, which is a closely related and complementary sector to the textiles and textile products sector. As also shown in Chapter 6, leather, leather products, and footwear is a sector that Bangladesh can easily jump to given its advantage in the textiles and textile products sector. Other products belong to the food, beverages, and tobacco sector; transport equipment sector; and the machinery, NEC sector. These sectors can also be examined to see if there is potential for Bangladesh to promote exports in and join the GVCs for these sectors.

Additionally, Table 6.1 also shows that the post and telecommunications sector, Bangladesh's second-ranked sector of RCA, is another sector Bangladesh can explore. This sector has a high forward GVC participation rate compared with the other sectors in the table, implying its large contribution to the re-exports of other economies. Another sector is the manufacturing, NEC sector, which has high backward and forward agglomeration indexes. As opposed to the textiles and textile products sector, this sector has high value-added capture in the domestic economy and a large role for domestic sectors in supporting domestic production in the sector.

It must be noted that if an economy currently shows no comparative disadvantage in sectors or products, it does not mean that it can never build advantage in that sector. Building competitiveness, modifying GVC participation and position, and tapping into agglomeration potential in different sectors and products will depend on the governments' strategic goals and the policies it implements to achieve these goals. As emphasized in earlier chapters, this has happened for the textiles and textile product sectors in the 1980s, and it must happen for the other sectors as well to achieve Vision 2041. Indeed, the Government of Bangladesh acknowledges that the policies it had put in place to succeed in RMG can be replicated for other manufacturing sectors as well (Bangladesh Planning Commission 2020). Additionally, Sattar (2022) and the Bangladesh Planning Commission (2020) pointed out that Bangladesh will need to overhaul its high tariff trade regime to lower the cost of imports and support other exporting sectors into becoming price-competitive in the world market. These tariffs will also come into play in the negotiations between Bangladesh and its partner economies to overcome the impending challenges to its exports.

Aside from sector and product concentration, Bangladesh also faces a narrow market for its exports. Chapter 5 showed that most of Bangladesh's exports go to the European Union and North America, thanks to the preferential schemes it enjoyed with these economies. With its graduation from least developed country status and the emergence of competitors like Viet Nam, these preferential schemes are under threat, and Bangladesh must look for alternative destinations that can absorb its exports. Building relationships and striking trade agreements with partner economies will be crucial in the coming years as Bangladesh pursues export-led economic growth and job creation.

As Chapter 6 pointed out, foreign direct investment (FDI) and digitalization can play a crucial role in transforming the Bangladesh economy and promoting exports and GVC participation. Key impediments to FDI in Bangladesh include inadequate physical infrastructure and skills development, sluggish judicial processes and dispute resolution, as well as bureaucratic delays and poor institutional quality (US DOS 2021). Quality institutions play an important role in ensuring that businesses can thrive in the economy and that policies are well-designed and efficiently and unbiasedly enacted. Quality institutions are also important in promoting entrepreneurship in and attracting FDI into priority export sectors while protecting those who may be disadvantaged by strategic policy changes. Horizontal policies on improving infrastructure, human capital development, and institutions can attract FDI into Bangladesh, but these need to be accompanied by sector-specific policies in the leather and leather product sectors as well as information and communication technology (ICT) and digital services for boosting and leveraging FDI for increasing sector exports and GVC participation.

Economic analysis in Chapter 6 suggests that digitalization of manufacturing firms is associated with higher export intensity and firm productivity. Thus, investments in digitalization-enabling infrastructure and firm-level digital capabilities can play a big part in promoting export-led growth in Bangladesh. Policies that even incrementally improve technologies in the apparel, leather, and footwear sector and the ICT sector can foster digital-led economic transformation in the country. However, the scope of digital-led transformation is narrowing due to a significant and widening digital divide between Bangladesh and its comparators. There is need for urgent investments in digital infrastructure, coupled with investments in improving the quality of education, financial deepening, and improving access to finance. The government's support in terms of specific policies for improving digital connectivity, data affordability, digital skills, and e-commerce logistics in the leather sector, coupled with firms' industrial capabilities gained from the success of the closely linked RMG sector, has important potential to kick-start export-led growth in Bangladesh's leather and leather products.

APPENDIXES

Appendix 1: Economies in the ADB Multiregional Input–Output Database

ID	Code	Economy	Region
1	AUS	Australia	Pacific
2	AUT	Austria	Europe
3	BEL	Belgium	Europe
4	BUL	Bulgaria	Europe
5	BRA	Brazil	Latin America and the Caribbean
6	CAN	Canada	North America
7	SWI	Switzerland	Europe
8	PRC	People's Republic of China	East Asia
9	CYP	Cyprus	Europe
10	CZE	Czech Republic	Europe
11	GER	Germany	Europe
12	DEN	Denmark	Europe
13	SPA	Spain	Europe
14	EST	Estonia	Europe
15	FIN	Finland	Europe
16	FRA	France	Europe
17	UKG	United Kingdom	Europe
18	GRC	Greece	Europe
19	HRV	Croatia	Europe
20	HUN	Hungary	Europe
21	INO	Indonesia	Southeast Asia
22	IND	India	South Asia
23	IRE	Ireland	Europe
24	ITA	Italy	Europe
25	ITA	Japan	East Asia
26	KOR	Republic of Korea	East Asia
27	LTU	Lithuania	Europe
28	LUX	Luxembourg	Europe
29	LVA	Latvia	Europe
30	MEX	Mexico	Latin America and the Caribbean
31	MLT	Malta	Europe
32	NET	Netherlands	Europe
33	NOR	Norway	Europe

continued on next page.

Appendix 1 *continued.*

ID	Code	Economy	Region
34	POL	Poland	Europe
35	POR	Portugal	Europe
36	ROU	Romania	Europe
37	RUS	Russian Federation	Europe
38	SVK	Slovak Republic	Europe
39	SVN	Slovenia	Europe
40	SWE	Sweden	Europe
41	TUR	Türkiye	Europe
42	TAP	Taipei,China	East Asia
43	USA	United States	North America
44	BAN	Bangladesh	South Asia
45	MAL	Malaysia	Southeast Asia
46	PHI	Philippines	Southeast Asia
47	THA	Thailand	Southeast Asia
48	VIE	Viet Nam	Southeast Asia
49	KAZ	Kazakhstan	Central and West Asia
50	MON	Mongolia	East Asia
51	SRI	Sri Lanka	South Asia
52	PAK	Pakistan	South Asia
53	FIJ	Fiji	Pacific
54	LAO	Lao People's Democratic Republic	Southeast Asia
55	BRU	Brunei Darussalam	Southeast Asia
56	BHU	Bhutan	South Asia
57	KGZ	Kyrgyz Republic	Central and West Asia
58	CAM	Cambodia	Southeast Asia
59	MLD	Maldives	South Asia
60	NEP	Nepal	South Asia
61	SIN	Singapore	Southeast Asia
62	HKG	Hong Kong, China	East Asia
63	ROW	Rest of the World	

Source: ADB. Multiregional Input–Output Database (accessed 14 July 2022).

Appendix 2: Sectors in the ADB Multiregional Input–Output Database

ID	35-Sector Aggregation	Short Name	Code	5-Sector Aggregation
1	Agriculture, hunting, forestry, and fishing	Agriculture	AHF	Primary
2	Mining and quarrying	Mining	MIN	Primary
3	Food, beverages, and tobacco	Food and beverages	FOO	Low-technology manufacturing
4	Textiles and textile products	Textiles	TEX	Low-technology manufacturing
5	Leather, leather products, and footwear	Leather and footwear	LEA	Low-technology manufacturing
6	Wood and products of wood and cork	Wood	WOO	Low-technology manufacturing
7	Pulp, paper, paper products, printing and publishing	Paper	PAP	Low-technology manufacturing
8	Coke, refined petroleum, and nuclear fuel	Refined fuels	FUE	Medium- to high-technology manufacturing
9	Chemicals and chemical products	Chemicals	CHE	Medium- to high-technology manufacturing
10	Rubber and plastics	Rubber and plastics	RUB	Low-technology manufacturing
11	Other nonmetallic minerals	Other minerals	OMN	Medium- to high-technology manufacturing
12	Basic metals and fabricated metal	Metals	MET	Medium- to high-technology manufacturing
13	Machinery, NEC	Machinery, NEC	MAC	Medium- to high-technology manufacturing
14	Electrical and optical equipment	Electricals	ELE	Medium- to high-technology manufacturing
15	Transport equipment	Transport equipment	TRA	Medium- to high-technology manufacturing
16	Manufacturing, NEC; recycling	Manufacturing, NEC	MAN	Low-technology manufacturing
17	Electricity, gas, and water supply	Utilities	UTL	Low-technology manufacturing
18	Construction	Construction	CON	Low-technology manufacturing
19	Sale, maintenance and repair of motor vehicles and motorcycles; retail sale of fuel	Sales of motor vehicles	VEH	Business services
20	Wholesale trade and commission trade, except of motor vehicles and motorcycles	Wholesale trade	WHO	Business services
21	Retail trade, except of motor vehicles and motorcycles; repair of household goods	Retail trade and repair	RET	Business services
22	Hotels and restaurants	Hotels and restaurants	HOT	Business services
23	Inland transport	Inland transport	ILT	Business services
24	Water transport	Water transport	WTR	Business services
25	Air transport	Air transport	AIR	Business services
26	Other supporting and auxiliary transport activities; activities of travel agencies	Other transport services	OTR	Business services
27	Post and telecommunications	Post and telecommunications	TEL	Business services
28	Financial intermediation	Finance	FIN	Business services
29	Real estate activities	Real estate	REA	Business services

continued on next page.

Appendix 2 *continued.*

ID	35-Sector Aggregation	Short Name	Code	5-Sector Aggregation
30	Renting of machinery and equipment and other business activities	Other business activities	OBA	Business services
31	Public administration and defense; compulsory social security	Public administration	PUB	Personal and public services
32	Education	Education	EDU	Personal and public services
33	Health and social work	Health and social work	HEA	Personal and public services
34	Other community, social and personal services	Other personal services	OPS	Personal and public services
35	Private households with employed persons	Private households	PHH	Personal and public services

NEC = not elsewhere classified.
Source: ADB. Multiregional Input–Output Database (accessed 14 July 2022).

REFERENCES

Ahmad, N. 2019. Chapter 8: Improving the Accounting Frameworks for Analyses of Global Value Chains. In World Bank and World Trade Organization. *Global Value Chain Development Report 2019: Technological Innovation, Supply Chain Trade and Workers in a Globalized World*. Washington, DC: World Bank.

Al Fattah, Md. A. 2020. How Cross Border E-commerce Can Revive Bangladesh RMG. *Daily Sun*. 12 May. https://www.daily-sun.com/arcprint/details/481419/How-cross-border-ecommerce-can-revive-Bangladesh-RMG/2020-05-12.

Andreoni, A. and S. Roberts. 2020. Governing Data and Digital Platforms in Middle Income Countries: Regulations, Competition and Industrial Policies, with Sectoral Case Studies from South Africa. *Digital Pathways Paper Series*. No. 5. Oxford: University of Oxford.

Asian Development Bank (ADB). 2018. Developing the Leather Industry in Bangladesh. *ADB Briefs*. No. 102. Manila.

ADB. 2021a. *Capturing the Digital Economy: A Proposed Measurement Framework and Its Applications*. A Special Supplement to *Key Indicators for Asia and the Pacific 2021*. Manila. https://www.adb.org/sites/default/files/publication/722366/capturing-digital-economy-measurement-framework.pdf.

ADB. 2021b. *Key Indicators for Asia and the Pacific 2021*. Manila.

ADB. 2022a. *Aid for Trade in Asia and the Pacific: Leveraging Trade and Digital Agreements for Sustainable Development*. Manila. https://www.adb.org/publications/aid-trade-asia-pacific-trade-digital-agreements.

ADB. 2022b. *Economic Insights from Input–Output Tables for Asia and the Pacific*. Manila.

ADB. 2022c. Multiregional Input-Output Database. http://mrio.adbx.online (accessed 14 July 2022 and 26 October 2022).

ASEAN Secretariat. Regional Comprehensive Economic Partnership (RCEP). https://rcepsec.org/about/.

Bajaj, P., K. V. Baris, P. G. B. Gonzales, C. R. Jabagat, J. E. Lazatin, and E. Tan. 2022. A Case for Value-Added Exports in the Estimation of Export Diversification in Asia and the Pacific. *ADB Economics Working Paper Series*. No. 650. Manila: ADB.

Balassa, B. 1965. Trade Liberalisation and "Revealed" Comparative Advantage. *The Manchester School*. 33 (2). pp. 99–123.

Banga, K. and M. Mendez-Parra. 2021. *Leveraging E-commerce in Bangladesh for Post-Crisis Recovery*. Bangladesh Trade Policy and Negotiation Capacity Building Support Project. London: Overseas Development Institute.

Banga, K. and D. W. te Velde. 2018. *Digitalisation and the Future of Manufacturing in Africa*. London: Overseas Development Institute.

Banga, R. and Banga, K., 2020. Digitalization and India's losing export competitiveness. Accelerators of India's Growth—Industry, Trade and Employment: Festschrift in Honor of Bishwanath Goldar, pp.129-158.

Banga, K., 2022. Digital technologies and product upgrading in global value chains: Empirical evidence from Indian manufacturing firms. *The European Journal of Development Research*, pp.1-26.

Bangladesh Bank, Statistics Department. 2022. Foreign Investment & External Debt Management Cell (accessed 5 October 2022).

Bangladesh Planning Commission, General Economics Division. 2020. *Making Vision 2041 a Reality: Perspective Plan of Bangladesh 2021–2041*. Dhaka. http://oldweb.lged.gov.bd/uploadeddocument/unitpublication/1/1049/vision%202021-2041.pdf.

Baris, K. V., M. C. R. Crisostomo, K. A. V. Garay, C. R. J. Jabagat, M. J. Mariasingham, and E. M. T. Mores. 2022. Measuring Localization in the Age of Economic Globalization. *ADB Economics Working Paper Series*. No. 647. Manila: ADB.

Bernard, A. B., J. B. Jensen, S. J. Redding, and P. K. Schott. 2007. Firms in International Trade. *Journal of Economic Perspectives*. 21 (3). pp. 105–130.

Borin, A. and M. Mancini. 2019. Measuring What Matters in Global Value Chains and Value-Added Trade. *Policy Research Working Paper*. No. 8804. Washington, DC: World Bank.

Broome, P. A. 2016. Conceptualizing the Foundations of a Regional E-commerce Strategy: Open Networks or Closed Regimes? The Case of CARICOM. *Cogent Business & Management*. 3 (1). 1139441.

Centre d'Etudes Prospectives d'Informations Internationales (CEPII). Basis for International Trade Analysis (BACI) International Trade Database (accessed 21 July 2022).

Choi, J., M. M. Hinojales, S. H. L. Hong, and J. Vichyanond. 2021. The Role of Vietnam's FDI Inflows in Global Value Chains Participation and Economic Growth. *AMRO Working Paper*. No. 21-02. https://www.amro-asia.org/wp-content/uploads/2021/05/The-Role-of-Vietnams-FDI-Inflows-in-Global-Value-Chains-Participation-and-Economic-Growth.pdf.

Crivelli, P. 2022. *Diversifying Global Value Chains* [Unpublished proposal].

References

Crivelli, P. and S. Inama. 2021. Improving Market for LDCs: The Impact of the EU Reform of Rules of Origin on Utilization Rates and Trade Flows under the Everything But Arms Initiative (EBA). *UN LDC5 Conference Paper.* https://www.un.org/ldc5/sites/www.un.org.ldc5/files/t6_inama_eu_reform_2021_16_helsinki_final_20210816_clean.pdf.

Duarte, M. and D. Restuccia. 2010. The Role of the Structural Transformation in Aggregate Productivity. *The Quarterly Journal of Economics.* 125 (1). pp.129–173.

Gaglio, C., Kraemer-Mbula, E. and Lorenz, E., 2022. The effects of digital transformation on innovation and productivity: Firm-level evidence of South African manufacturing micro and small enterprises. *Technological Forecasting and Social Change.* 182, 121785.

Government of Canada. 2022. About the Comprehensive and Progressive Agreement for Trans-Pacific Partnership. https://www.international.gc.ca/trade-commerce/trade-agreements-accords-commerciaux/agr-acc/cptpp-ptpgp/backgrounder-document_information.aspx?lang=eng.

Grossman, G. and E. Rossi- Hansberg. 2008. Trading Tasks: A Simple Theory of Offshoring. *American Economic Review.* 98 (5). p.1978–1997.

Gu, Y., G. Nayyar, and S. Sharma. 2021. *Gearing Up for the Future of Manufacturing in Bangladesh.* Washington, DC: World Bank. https://openknowledge.worldbank.org/handle/10986/35879.

Hallward-Driemeier, M. and G. Nayyar. 2017. *Trouble in the Making?: The Future of Manufacturing-Led Development.* Washington, DC: World Bank.

Hallward-Driemeier, M. and G. Nayyar. 2019. Have Robots Grounded the Flying Geese?: Evidence from Greenfield FDI in Manufacturing. Evidence from Greenfield FDI in Manufacturing. *Policy Research Working Paper.* No. 9097. Washington, DC: World Bank.

Hasan, I., M. N. Islam, and S. R. Khan. 2020. Ready-Made Garment Industry Attractiveness: The Case of Bangladesh Garments' Blue-Collar Employees. *International Journal of Emerging Markets.* 17 (5). pp. 1218–1237. https://doi.org/10.1108/IJOEM-03-2019-0232.

Hidalgo, C. A., B. Klinger, A. L. Barabási, and R. Hausmann. 2007. The Product Space Conditions the Development of Nations. *Science.* 317 (5837). pp. 482–487.

Hing, V., Thangavelu, S.M. and Kong, R., 2023. Technology, Innovation, and Firm Competitiveness: Firm Level Analysis in Cambodia.

Hjort, J. and J. Poulsen. 2019. The Arrival of Fast Internet and Employment in Africa. *American Economic Review.* 109 (3). pp.1032–1079.

Hummels, D., J. Ishii, and K. M. Yi. 2001. The Nature and Growth of Vertical Specialization in World Trade. *Journal of International Economics.* 54 (1). pp. 75–96.

International Labour Organization (ILO). 2022. ILOSTAT Database (accessed 29 November 2022).

International Monetary Fund (IMF). 2022. World Economic Outlook Database: April 2022 edition (accessed 11 August 2022).

International Telecommunication Union. 2022. ICT Digital Development Dashboard (accessed 5 November 2022).

International Trade Centre (ITC). 2018. *What Sells in E-commerce: New Evidence from Asian LDCs*. Geneva.

Kumar, D. 2022. Developing Regional Value Chains in the Textile and Garment Sector of South Asia. *South and South-West Asia Development Papers*. No. 22-05. New Delhi: United Nations Economic and Social Commission for Asia and the Pacific (UNESCAP).

Kummritz, V. 2016. Do Global Value Chains Cause Industrial Development? *CTEI Working Papers*. No. 01-2016. Geneva: Centre for Trade and Economic Integration.

Matthess, M. and S. Kunkel. 2020. Structural Change and Digitalization in Developing Countries: Conceptually Linking the Two Transformations. *Technology in Society*. 63. 101428. https://doi.org/10.1016/j.techsoc.2020.101428.

McMillan, M., D. Rodrik, and Í. Verduzco-Gallo. 2014. Globalization, Structural Change, and Productivity Growth, with an Update on Africa. *World Development*. Elsevier. 63. pp.11–32.

Mercer-Blackman, V., A. S. Foronda, and M. Mariasingham. 2017. Using Input-Output Analysis Framework to Explain Economic Diversification and Structural Transformation in Bangladesh. *ADB Economics Working Paper Series*. No. 513. Manila: ADB.

Newfarmer, R., J. Page, and F. Tarp. 2019. *Industries Without Smokestacks: Industrialization in Africa Reconsidered*. Oxford University Press. p. 480.

Raihan, S. and S. S. Khan. 2020. Structural Transformation, Inequality Dynamics, and Inclusive Growth in Bangladesh. *WIDER Working Paper*. No. 2020/44. Helsinki, Finland: United Nations University World Institute for Development Economics Research.

Razzaque, M. A., A. Eusuf, M. Uddin, and J. Rahman. 2020. Exports of Leather and Leather Goods: Performance, Prospects, and Policy Priorities. In M. A. Razzaque, ed. *Navigating New Waters: Unleashing Bangladesh's Export Potential for Smooth LDC Graduation*. Dhaka: Bangladesh Enterprise Institute. pp. 229–266.

Rodrik, D. 2013. Unconditional Convergence in Manufacturing. *Quarterly Journal of Economies*. 128 (1). pp. 165–204.

Rodrik, D. 2018. New Technologies, Global Value Chains, and Developing Economies. *NBER Working Paper*. No. 25164. Cambridge, MA: National Bureau of Economic Research.

Sattar, Z. 2022. The Rise of Readymade Garment Industry: Still a Beacon of Hope for Bangladesh. *Policy Insights*. 26 June. https://policyinsightsonline.com/2022/06/the-rise-of-readymade-garment-industry-still-a-beacon-of-hope-for-bangladesh/.

Sattar, Z. and Z. Ahmed. 2021. *Post-COVID19 Export Development Strategy for Bangladesh*. Bangladesh Trade Policy and Negotiation Capacity Building Support Project. London: Overseas Development Institute. http://pri-odi-tradenegotiaitons-capacitybuilding-taf2-moc.com/wp-content/uploads/2021/03/Export-Development-Strategy-Post-Covid-19.pdf.

Shepherd, B. 2015. Product Standards and Export Diversification. *Journal of Economic Integration*. 30(2). pp. 300–333

Shepherd, B. 2020. Firm Size and Participation in the International Economy: Evidence from Bangladesh. *ADB Working Paper Series*. No. 1119. Manila: ADB.

Sturgeon, T. J. 2021. Upgrading Strategies for the Digital Economy. *Global Strategy Journal*. 11 (1). pp. 34–57.

Swazan, I. S. and D. Das. 2022. Bangladesh's Emergence as a Ready-Made Garment Export Leader: An Examination of the Competitive Advantages of the Garment Industry. *International Journal of Global Business and Competitiveness*. 17 (2). pp. 162–174.

Taglioni, D. and D. Winkler. 2016. *Making Global Value Chains Work for Development*. Washington, DC: The World Bank.

The Business Standard. 2020. Covid-19: E-commerce Facing Tk666 Crore Losses per Month. 13 May. https://www.tbsnews.net/economy/covid-19-e-commerce-facing-tk666-crore-losses-month-81061.

The Growth Lab at Harvard University. N.d. The Atlas of Economic Complexity. http://www.atlas.cid.harvard.edu.

The Growth Lab at Harvard University. 2019a. Growth Projections and Complexity Rankings. V3. Harvard Dataverse (accessed 18 November 2022).

The Growth Lab at Harvard University. 2019b. International Trade Data (HS, 92). V5. Harvard Dataverse (accessed 18 November 2022).

United Nations Conference on Trade and Development (UNCTAD). 2021a. The UNCTAD B2C E-commerce Index 2020: Spotlight on Latin America and the Caribbean. *UNCTAD Technical Notes on ICT for Development*. No. 17. Geneva. https://unctad.org/system/files/official-document/tn_unctad_ict4d17_en.pdf.

UNCTAD. 2021b. Getting to Better Rules of Origin for LDCs Using Utilization Rates. Geneva. https://unctad.org/system/files/official-document/aldc2019d3_en.pdf.

UNCTAD. 2021c. Generalized System of Preferences - Handbook on the Scheme of Canada, 3rd Edition. Geneva. https://unctad.org/system/files/official-document/itcdtsbmisc66rev2_en.pdf.

UNCTAD. UNCTADstat (accessed 10 November 2022).

United Nations University World Institute for Development Economics Research. 2022. Economic Transformation Database (accessed 15 October 2022).

United States Department of State. 2021. *2021 Investment Climate Statements: Bangladesh*. https://www.state.gov/reports/2021-investment-climate-statements/bangladesh/.

Wang, Z., S. Wei, X. Yu, and K. Zhu. 2017a. Characterizing Global Value Chains: Production Length and Upstreamness. *NBER Working Paper*. No. 23261. Cambridge, MA: National Bureau of Economic Research.

Wang, Z., S. Wei, X. Yu, and K. Zhu. 2017b. Measures of Participation in Global Value Chains and Global Business Cycles. *NBER Working Paper*. No. 23222. Cambridge, MA: National Bureau of Economic Research.

Woodruff, C. 2014. Managing for Efficiency in the Garment Sector. In D. W. te Velde, ed. *Enhancing Productivity in Bangladesh's Garment Sector: Current Policy and Research Debates*. DFID-ESRC Growth Programme (DEGRP).

World Bank. 2007. Enterprise Survey 2007, Bangladesh (accessed 5 October 2022).

World Bank. 2011. Enterprise Survey 2011, Bangladesh (accessed 5 October 2022).

World Bank. 2013. Enterprise Survey 2013, Bangladesh (accessed 5 October 2022).

World Bank. 2018. Logistics Performance Index Dataset (accessed 29 November 2022).

World Bank. 2022. World Development Indicators (accessed 11 August 2022, 17 October 2022, and 21 November 2022).

World Trade Organization. 2019. Trade in Services Data by Mode of Supply (TISMOS) (accessed 10 November 2022).

Yu, R., J. Cai, and P. S. Leung. 2009. The Normalized Revealed Comparative Advantage Index. *Annals of Regional Science*. 43 (1). pp. 267–282.

Zaman, S. 2021. Researching the Garment Sector in Bangladesh: Fieldwork Challenges and Responses. In M. R. Islam et al., eds. *Field Guide for Research in Community Settings*. Cheltenham, UK: Edward Elgar Publishing. pp. 75–84.